BRAHMAN

A STUDY

IN THE

HISTORY OF INDIAN PHILOSOPHY

BRAHMAN

A STUDY

IN THE

HISTORY OF INDIAN PHILOSOPHY

HERVEY DEWITT GRISWOLD

GYAN

Published by

Gyan Publishing House
5, Ansari Road
Daryaganj, New Delhi-110002
Phone: 011-47034999, 9811692060
E-mail: books@gyanbooks.com

Distribution Network
gyanbooks.com
India, USA, Canada, UK, Australia

ISBN: 978-93-6780-261-8 (PB)

First Published, 1900

2nd Impression 2024

Printed at: Gyan Press, Delhi.

BRAHMAN A STUDY ON THE HISTORY OF INDIAN PHILOSOPHY
Author: HERVEY DEWITT GRISWOLD

CORNELL STUDIES IN PHILOSOPHY

No. 2

BRAHMAN:

A STUDY

IN THE

HISTORY OF INDIAN PHILOSOPHY

BY

HERVEY DEWITT GRISWOLD, M.A.

Fellow of the Panjâb University and Professor of Philosophy in the Forman Christian College, Lahore.

New York

THE MACMILLAN COMPANY

1900

PREFACE.

TWO countries share the honor of being the birthplaces of the chief historic religions of the world, Palestine-Arabia and India. The one is the ancestral home of Judaism, Christianity, and Islâm; the other, of Brahmanism and Buddhism. Genetically, Judaism is the mother of both Christianity and Mohammedanism, as Brahmanism is the mother of Buddhism. Buddhism, Christianity, and Mohammedanism belong to the class of instituted religions, in that they go back into great creative personalities, after which they are respectively named; whereas Judaism and Brahmanism, the mother religions of the world, are properly characterized as spontaneous, since they have their origin in the tribe rather than in the individual. The one allied group of religions, namely Judaism, Christianity, and Islâm, grew up and made its earliest conquests in the region having the Mediterranean for its center. The other group, represented by Brahmanism and Buddhism, appeared and spread in India-China and the neighboring regions, the second ancient center of the world's civilization. The sacred language of Judaism is Hebrew, and the sacred language of Brahmanism, Sanskrit. Hence both linguistically and racially the western group springs from a Semitic source, while the eastern springs from an Aryan source. Thus the history of religion has to do primarily with two geographical centers, Palestine and India; with two races, Semitic and Aryan; and with two languages, Hebrew and Sanskrit.

In this monograph I purpose to make a special study of the doctrine of Bráhman, the central conception of Indian philosophy and religion. Accordingly, it will be a study both in the history of philosophy and in the history of religion. The method will be genetic and comparative. It will be genetic, for the conception of Brahman will be traced through the Vedas, the Upanishads, the Vedânta-Sûtras, and the Commentary of Çankarâcârya. It will be comparative, for the religious aspects of the doctrine of

Brahman will constantly be illustrated by the parallel development in Judaism and Christianity; while the philosophical aspects of the doctrine will, at least in their main features, be set side by side with the corresponding ideas in the ancient and modern philosophy of the West.

The importance of the conception of Brahman in the history of Indian thought is indicated by the fact that the word 'Brahman' has supplied the name to (1) a class of priests, the Brâhmans; (2) a department of ancient Sanskrit literature, the *Brâhmaṇas*; (3) the Ultimate Reality of the Vedânta, Brahma; (4) the first person of the later Hindu Trinity, Brahmâ; (5) Indian religion before the Buddhist disruption, Brahmanism, and (6) the modern theistic movement known as the Brahma Samâj.

It will, of course, be possible to deal only with the main outlines of the doctrine of Brahman. For, as Professor Flint truly says, to explain in detail the how and why of the development of the doctrine of Brahman would be to write the longest chapter in the history of Hindu civilization.[1]

As regards literature, my largest indebtedness is to the works of Professor Deussen, especially to his *Allgemeine Geschichte der Philosophie, erster Band*, which deals with the philosophy of the pre-Upanishad period, and to his *Sechzig Upanishads des Veda*. Prof. Max Mueller's *Six Systems of Indian Philosophy*, and Professor Thibaut's careful translation of the Vedânta-Sûtras (SBE. vols. XXXIV and XXXVIII) have also been of very great service. Col. Jacob's *Concordance to the Upanishads* is, of course, indispensable to every worker in the field of the Upanishads.

The method of transliteration used is essentially the same as that found in Professor Whitney's Sanskrit Grammar. I must plead guilty, however, of not always following it consistently. Words such as *upanishad*, *rishi*, *purusha*, *prakriti*, etc., have become anglicized, and so I have not always written them as *upaniṣad*, *ṛṣi*, *puruṣa* and *prakṛti*. I have written s in the place of visarga.

The development of the doctrine of Bráhman (neuter as opposed to Brahmán) is indicated by three well marked stages: (*a*) the initial or germinal stage represented by the Rig-Veda, the

[1] *Anti-Theistic Theories*, p. 344.

Atharva-Veda and the early prose, excluding the Upanishads; (*b*) the stage of creative thought represented by the Upanishads; and (*c*) the stage of system building and exposition represented by the Vedânta-Sûtras, as expounded by Çankarâcârya. To these a fourth stage might be added, namely, that of Indian scholasticism and theological subtlety, as illustrated by the later doctrinal treatises, *e. g.*, the *Vedânta Sâra* and the *Vedânta Paribhâṣâ.* These stages, I say, are well marked, not indeed by external chronological data, which in India are almost entirely lacking, but by what has been happily called internal chronology, the chronology of language and thought. Thus even the language reveals three clearly marked stages of development, Vedic, Brâhmanic, and Classic. The absolute dates of the *Rig-Veda*, of the *Brâhmaṇas*, and of the beginnings of Classic Sanskrit in the Sûtra period, are very uncertain, and yet their respective places in the development of Sanskrit literature are sufficiently clear and definite. It is to be noted that the three stages in the development of the doctrine of Bráhman, namely, initial, creative, and systematic, correspond in general to the three periods in the history of the language, Vedic, Brâhmanic, and Classic.

It is only when we come to the Upanishads that Bráhman uniformly means the Ultimate Reality. Doubtless centuries of language and thought development elapsed before the word bráhman and the idea which was finally associated with this word came to be integrated. Two streams, then, are to be traced down from their sources until they meet and flow together; one represented by the word 'bráhman' with its development and flow of meaning, the other consisting of the idea of the Sole Reality as it variously manifests itself in the early literature. Or, to state it differently, we have first to trace the preparation of the word for the idea, and of the idea for the word. This will involve, on the one hand, a study of the derivation and use of the word 'brahman,' and, on the other, some account of the course of Vedic thought as it gradually moved towards a unitary conception of things.

CONTENTS.

LIST OF ABBREVIATIONS.

Ait. Âr.........*Aitareya Âraṇyaka.*
Ait. Br..........*Aitareya Brâhmaṇa.*
Altind. Gram...Altindische Grammatik—Wackernagel, 1896.
Apocal. Ioh.....Apocalypse of John.
Av..............Avesta.
AV..............Atharva-Veda.
Bṛh Up.........*Bṛhadâraṇyaka Upanishad.*
Buddha..........Buddha: His Life, His Doctrine, His Order. Oldenberg (Eng. Trans. by Hoey, Lond., 1882).
Comp. Gram....Comparative Grammar of the Indo-Germanic Languages—Brugmann. (Eng. Trans.).
Çat. Br.........*Çatapatha Brâhmaṇa.*
Çvet. Up........Çvetâçvatara Upanishad.
Chând. Up......Chândogya Upanishad.
Essays..........Essays on the Religion and Philosophy of the Hindus—H. T. Colebrooke (Leipzig, 1858).
Evang. Ioh.....Gospel of John.
Geschichte......Allgemeine Geschichte der Philosophie.
IE...............Indo-European.
Kaush. Up......Kaushîtaki Upanishad.
Kultur...........Indiens Literatur and Kultur—Schroeder.
Mac.............Maccabees.
Mait. Up........*Maitrâyaṇa Upanishad.*
Manuel..........Manuel de la Langue de l'Avesta—De Harlez (Paris 1882).
N. T............New Testament.
OST.............Original Sanskrit Texts.
O. T.............Old Testament.
Ps...............Psalm.
RV...............Rig-Veda.
Roots...........The Roots, Verb-forms and primary derivatives of the Sanskrit Language—Whitney.
SBE.............Sacred Books of the East.
Six Systems....The Six Systems of Indian Philosophy--Max Müller.
Taitt. Up.......Taittirîya Upanishad.
Taitt. Saṁh... *Taittirîya Saṁhitâ.*
Upanishads.....Sechzig Upanishads des Veda.
Vâj. Saṁh..... *Vâjasaneyi Saṁhitâ.*
Veda............Die Religion des Veda—Oldenberg.
Vedânta.........Das System des Vedânta—Deussen.
LDMG...........Zeitschrift der Deutschen Morgenländischen Gesellschaft.

CHAPTER I.

The History of the Word Bráhman.

The word '*bráhman*' is the greatest word in the whole history of Indian Philosophy. On it hangs largely the development of Indian thought. The meanings assigned to it are numerous and bewildering. It has been explained and translated by such various terms as worship, devotion, fervor, prayer, hymn, charm, incantation, sanctity, holiness, priesthood, spiritual exaltation, sacred writ, Veda, Vedic formula, priestly order, holy work, priestly dignity, inspiration, force, spiritual power, ultimate reality, absolute. Thus it seems to mean almost anything. On the principle that accuracy of thought depends upon the accurate understanding and use of the words which are the instruments of thought, in other words that sound thinking presupposes sound philology, we are justified in taking some trouble to determine the history of the word '*bráhman*.'

A. Usage of Bráhman.

We shall consider the actual usage of the word before its etymology, in order, if possible, to be delivered from the vice of a one-sided etymologizing. First, then, the word '*bráhman*' in the Rig-Veda. According to Grassmann's Index Lexicon it occurs in the RV. about 240 times. A careful study of these passages yields the following results: (1) The word '*bráhman*' frequently stands side by side in the same *pâda* or foot with one or more names for hymn, *e. g.*, *stoma*, *uktha*, *dhî*, etc., presumably as a general synonym. *E. g.*, II, 39, 8 (*bráhma stomam*), *i. e.*

These means of strength for you, O heavenly horsemen,
Bráhman (and) praise-song made the Gritsamadas.

VI, 23, 1 (*stoma bráhman uktha*), *i. e.*

The pressed out soma thou dost love, O Indra,
Bráhman (and) song of praise (and) hymn intonéd.

VI, 38, 3 (*bráhma ca giras*):
    Bráhman and psalms to Indra have been offered.
VI, 38, 4 (*bráhma gira ukthâ ca manma*).
    As sacrifice and *soma* strengthen Indra,
    So also *bráhman*, psalms and hymns and wisdom.

Compare also I, 80, 16 (*bráhmâṇi uktha*), VI, 47, 14 (*giro brahmâṇi*), VI, 69, 4 (*brahmâṇi . . . giraḥ*), VI, 69, 7 (*brahmâṇi . . . havam*), etc.

(2) The word '*bráhman*' also not infrequently stands over against some word for hymn in a different pâda of the same verse, doubtless in *synonymous parallelism* after the manner of Hebrew and Anglo-Saxon poetry. *E. g.*, VI, 38, 3–4 (*dhiyâ . . . arkâis——bráhmâ . . . giras*):

    With a high song of praise the ancient Indra
    Who ages not, with holy hymns I welcome;
    Bráhman and psalms to Indra have been offered,
    Oh may the glorious song of praise refresh him.

VI, 69, 4 (*havanâ matînâm* parallel with *brahmâṇi giras*),
    Be pleased with every cry of sacred worship,
    Hearken to my *brahmâṇi* and my praise-songs.[1]
VII, 61, 6 (*manmâni navâni* parallel with *brahma imâni*),
    May these new songs be unto you for praise-songs,
    May these *brahmâṇi* by me offered please you.

Compare also VII, 61, 2 (*manmâni* parallel with *brahmâṇi*), VII, 22, 3 (*vâcam imâm* parallel with *imâ brahma*), VII, 72, 3 (*stomâsas* parallel with *brahmâṇi*).

(3) The word '*bráhman*' frequently stands in the last verse of a hymn in such a way as clearly to refer to the preceding verses, *i. e.*, to the whole hymn. *E. g.*, I, 61, 16, I, 62, 13, I, 80, 16, I, 117, 25, I, 152, 7, IV, 6, 11, IV, 16, 21, V, 29, 15, V, 75, 19, VII, 22, 9, VII, 28, 5, X, 54, 6, X, 80, 7, etc. Note that of the group IV, 16–17, 19–24, each hymn ends in a kind of refrain which contains the words '*bráhma navyam*,' 'a new *bráhman*.'

(4) A limiting pronoun is sometimes added to '*bráhman*,' whether it stands in the last verse or not, in order apparently to

[1] Cf. Ps. CII, 1. "Hear my *prayer*, O Lord,
And let my *cry* come unto Thee."

make the reference to the hymn more explicit. *E. g.*, I, 31, 18 'Through this *bráhman*, Agni, be strengthened'; I, 152, 7 'our *bráhman*'; I, 165, 14, V, 73, 10, VII, 22, 3, VII, 61, 6, VII, 70, 6 'these *brahmâṇi*'; II, 18, 7 'my *bráhman*'; II, 34, 6 'our *brahmâṇi*'; II, 39, 8 'these *bráhman* (and) *stomá*'; VI, 69, 4 'my *brahmâṇi* (and) songs'; VI, 69, 7 'my *brahmâṇi* (and) cry.' Compare *imâm vâcam* 'this word' I, 40, 6, I, 129, 1, I, 130, 6, IV, 57, 5, V, 54, 1, VII, 22, 3, IX, 97, 13.

(5) The poets are said to have *fashioned* (*takṣ* I, 62, 13, V, 73, 10, X, 80, 7) and *generated* (*jan* II, 23, 2, VII, 22, 9, VII, 31, 11) the *bráhman*, just as they are described as fashioning or generating a *dhî* or *stoma* or *uktha* or *vâc* (I, 109, 1, V, 2, 11, VII, 15, 4, VII, 26, 1, X, 23, 6, X, 39, 14, I, 130, 6). Examples: I, 62, 13 'Gotama has fashioned a new *bráhman*.' Cf. I, 109, 1 'I have fashioned a *dhî* (hymn of meditation); VII. 31, 11 'The poets generated a *bráhman*.' Cf. VII, 15, 4 'A new *stoma* (song of praise) have I generated.'

(6) The word '*bráhman*' is joined with the verb *gâyata* 'sing' in I, 37, 4 and VIII, 32, 27 'Sing a god-given *bráhman*.' In VI, 69, 4 and 7 the gods are entreated to hear the *brahmâṇi*.

(7) The epithet 'new' is often applied to *bráhman* just as in VII, 15, 4, VIII, 23, 14 to *stoma*, in VII, 61, 6 to *manman*, and in II, 24, 1 to *gir*. Thus I, 62, 13, IV. 16, 21, V, 29, 15, VI, 17, 13, VI, 50, 6, VII, 61, 6, X, 89, 3. With the '*bráhma navyam*' of these and other passages compare the 'new song' of Pss. XL, 3, XCVI, 1, XCVIII, 1, etc.

(8) The adjective *abrahman* (without a *bráhman*) occurs three times: IV, 16, 9 *abrahmâ dasyus*, 'the *dasyu* without a *bráhman*'; VII, 26, 1 *abrahmâṇas sutâsas*, 'Libations without a *bráhman* do not exhilarate Indra'; X, 105, 8 'With a hymn (*ṛcâ*) may we overcome the hymnless (*anṛcaḥ*). A sacrifice without a *bráhman* (*abrahmâ*) does not please thee well.' Compare *abrahman* IV, 16, 9 with *anṛc* X, 105, 8.

(9) The idea of the inspiration of the hymn-writers, as Deussen observes,[1] is well developed in the Rig-Veda. Thus, I, 37, 4 'Sing a god-given (*devattam*) *bráhman*'; I, 105, 15 'Varuna

[1] *Allgemeine Geschichte der Philosophie*, S. 242 ff.

causes *brahmâṇi* . . . He reveals through our heart (*hṛdâ*) the sacred hymn (*mati*)'; II, 9, 4 'Thou art (O Agni) the deviser (*manotar*) of the splendid hymn (*vacas*)'; III, 34, 5 '(Indra) showed these hymns (*dhiyas*) to the singer'; IV, 11, 3 'From thee, Agni, come the gifts of sacred song; from thee hymns (*manîṣâs*) and holy texts (*ukthâ*)'; V, 42, 4 'Enrich us, Indra, with such a *bráhman* as is god-granted (*devahitam*)'; VI, 1, 1 'Thou, Agni, wast the first deviser of this sacred meditation (*dhî*)'; VII, 97, 3 '(Indra) who is the king of the god-made (*devakṛtasya*) *bráhman*'; VIII, 42, 3 'O Varuna, sharpen this hymn (*dhî*)'; IX, 95, 2 'The god (Soma) reveals the hidden names (attributes) of the gods'; X, 98, 7 'Brihaspati brought him the word (*vâc*).' Note also that in II, 23, 1 Bráhmanaspáti is called 'the great king of the *brahmâṇi*' and in v. 2 'the generator of *brahmâṇi*,' while in X, 61, 7 it is written: 'The gods generated *bráhman*.' Observe the entire parallelism as regards inspiration which exists between *bráhman* and its (presumable) synonyms, *mati*, *vacas*, *dhî*, *manîṣâ*, *uktha* and *vâc*.

(10) The efficacy of *bráhman* is represented as similar to that of *dhî*, *mantra*, *arka*, etc. *E. g.*, VII, 19, 11 'Quickened by *bráhman* (*brahma jûtas*), be strong in body (O Indra).' Cf. IX, 64, 16 'Quickened by the hymn (*dhiyâ jûtâs*), the soma-drops are poured forth.' V, 40, 6 'Atri with the fourth *bráhman* discovered the sun hidden by unholy darkness.' Cf. I, 67, 3 '(Agni) upheld the heavens by means of true mantras.' II, 24, 3 '(Brihaspati) smote Vala through *bráhman*.' Cf. V, 31, 4 'The priests magnifying Indra with hymns (*arka*) strengthened him for slaying the serpent.' Note also III, 53, 12 'The *bráhman* of Viçvamitra protects the tribe of Bharata'; VI, 75, 19 '*Bráhman* is my protecting armour'; VII, 33, 3 'Through your *bráhman*, O Vasishtha, Indra helped Sudâs in the battle of the ten kings.'[1] In X, 162, 1–2 the wish is expressed that Agni be united with *brahman* in order to expell illness.

What, then, is the meaning of *bráhman* in these representative passages? From the facts presented above it is evident that *bráhman* is a name for *hymn*, as it is used interchangeably for

[1] Cf. 1 Sam. VII, 8–9.

mantra, mati, manman, manîṣâ, dhî, stoma, arka, ṛc, gir, vacas, uktha, vâc, etc., all of which are applied as names to the Vedic hymns. When used in the plural *bráhman* seems to refer to a hymn as made up of a collection of verses. This suggests that in its earliest use *bráhman* may have referred to a single brief utterance of the priest in worship. A group of such utterances might be called either distributively *brahmâṇi* or collectively *bráhman*. The essentials of Vedic worship were sacrifice and *bráhman*. Both alike were means of quickening and strengthening the gods. Indeed, both were offerings, the one material consisting of *soma*, ghee, etc., the other spiritual, the sacrifice of prayer and praise. No worship was complete without *bráhman*, the sacred utterance. *Bráhman* may be rendered 'prayer,' provided that the word prayer be taken in a purely ritualistic and formal sense. It is not prayer in general, uttered or unuttered, stated or occasional, but rather "das rituell fixirte Gebet" (Oldenberg),[1] "das ausgesprochene Gebet, sei es Preis, Dank oder Bitte" (Grassmann), or in general, as defined by Roth in the St. Petersburg Lexicon, "jede fromme Aeusserung beim Gottesdienst." It is "the holy word"[2] (Bloomfield) which as used in the ritual becomes about equal to "prayer." So far as usage is concerned, *bráhman* might be rendered by 'hymn' as well as by 'prayer'; or, on the other hand, the synonyms of *bráhman*, viz, *mantra, vâc, stoma*, etc., might all be brought under the category of prayer, as is actually the procedure of Bergaigné.[3] Indeed Muir,[4] as the result of his inductive study of Vedic passages gives the alternative meaning "hymn or prayer." In the ritualistic stages of religion there is no essential difference between hymn and prayer. Both are chanted, and the emphasis rests not so much on inner content as on exactitude of liturgical use.

Secondly, *bráhman* in the *Atharva-Veda* and the *Brâhmaṇas*. These together with the Yajur-Veda constitute the chief literary documents of the *Brâhmaṇa* period. The texts quoted above under (10) concerning the magical efficacy of brahman, indicate

[1] *Veda*, S. 433.

[2] In a letter from Rev. A. H. Ewing, a pupil of Professor Bloomfield.

[3] *La religion védique*, p. 277.

[4] OST., Vol. I, p. 242.

the transition from the standpoint of the RV. to that of the AV., in which brahman frequently means *magic* formula or charm. As examples note the following texts as translated by Bloomfield[1]: I, 10, 1, 'From the wrath of the mighty do I, excelling in my incantation (*bráhman*), lead out this man'; I, 14, 4 'With the incantation (*bráhman*) of Asita . . . do I cover up thy fortune'; I, 23, 4 'The leprosy . . . I have destroyed with my charm (*bráhman*)'; II, 10, 1 'Guiltless do I render thee through my charm (*bráhman*)'; III, 6, 8 'I drive them out with my mind, drive them out with my thought, and also with my incantation (*bráhman*).' In harmony with the above texts is the fact that the Atharva-Veda is also called the Brahma-Veda, either from a schematic motive in order that the Brâhman-priests might have a Veda as well as the other three classes of priests, or because it is the Veda of *brahmâṇi*, *i. e.*, potent texts, spells, magical formulas. AV. XV, 6, 3[2] might serve as a proof text for the latter view. The same usage is found, though less often, in the other literature of the period, *e. g.*, Çat. Br.[3] I, 1, 2, 4 'He by this very prayer (or charm, *bráhman*) renders the atmosphere free from danger and evil spirits'; I, 7, 1, 8 'He thus makes over the sacrificer's cattle to it for protection by means of the *bráhman*.' See also *Vâj. Saṁh.* XI, 82 'I destroy the enemies by means of *bráhman*' (where *bráhman* is explained by the commentator Mahîdhara as the power of the *mantra* or charm). It is evident from the above quoted passages that bibliolatry, or the superstitious use of sacred texts, was common enough in the Vedic age.

Another meaning of bráhman, essentially the same as the two meanings already given, is sacred formula or text. Thus: Çat. Br. I, 5, 4, 6, 'Let us try to overcome one another by speech, by sacred writ (*vâc bráhman*)'; II, 1, 4, 10 'The *bráhman* is speech (*vâc*)'; I, 3, 1, 3, 'The bráhman is the sacrificial formula' (*bráhma yajus*); IV, 5, 2, 10 'This one he maks fit for the sacrifice by means of the *bráhman*, the *yajus*'; VII, 1, 1, 5 'The bráhman is the *mantra*'; IV, 1, 1, 4 'The bráhman is the *Gâyatrî*'; *Taitt.*

[1] SBE., Vol. XLII.

[2] *ṛcaç ca sâmâni ca yajûṇṣi ca brahma ca.*

[3] As translated by Eggeling (SBE. Vols. XII, XXVI, XLI, XLIII and XLIV).

Saṁh. VI, 1, 6, 6 'The Gandharvas were speaking the *bráhman*, the gods were chanting it.' So sacred is the bráhman that it constitutes the very speech of heaven.

Thus far we have found really only one meaning for the word 'bráhman.' In all the passages considered, whether in *Saṁhitâ* or *Brâhmaṇa*, it is in general 'the holy word.' The emphasis, however, at different times and in different texts rests upon different elements in the connotation of bráhman. Thus in the *Rig-Veda* it is the form and the function of bráhman that receive the emphasis—the form well wrought like a chariot and the function to strengthen and refresh the gods; in the *Atharva-Veda*, it is the power and potency of bráhman; while in the *Brâhmaṇas*, it is the element of sacredness due to the divine origin, antiquity, efficacy, and religious use of bráhman. In fact, we have here three moments in the Indian doctrine of Holy Scripture.

Hitherto we have considered the form and potency and sacredness of bráhman, the holy word, viewed as something consisting of hymn and sacred text, and so external and objective. But 'the holy word' may be taken in a more internal and subjective sense, as the truth, the inner content, the sacred doctrine, the wisdom and theology, of the external word. Thus, as representing the "theoretical side" (Roth) of religion, bráhman stands over against *tapas* 'austerity,' the practical side; just as in the N. T. faith (which includes knowledge) stands over against works. *E. g.*, AV. VI, 133, 3, VIII, 10, 25 'The seven Rishis live by *bráhman* and *tapas*'; XII, 1, 1 'Truth greatness . . . *tapas*, *bráhman*, sacrifice, support the earth'; Çat. Br. II, 1, 4, 10 'The *bráhman* is the truth (*satyam*).' In the Çat. Br. bráhman is defined in some passages by *trayî vidyâ*, 'the triple science' (*i. e.*, the combined doctrine of Rik, Sâma and Yajus). *E. g.*, VI, 1, 1, 8 'He created first of all the *bráhman*, the triple science'; II, 6, 4, 2–7 'With the *bráhman*, the triple science they encompassed them.' For the meaning of 'triple science' cf. I. 1, 4, 3 'The triple science is sacrifice' (the great doctrine of the three Vedas); IX, 3, 3, 14 'The Stoma, and the Yajus, and the Rik, and the Sâman, and the Brihat and the Rathantara (*i. e.*, the verses and meters of all the Vedas)—this, doubtless is the triple science'; X, 4, 2, 21 'He . . . beheld all existing things in the triple science, for therein is the body of all meters, of all stomas, of all vital airs, and of all the gods.'

We must now return to the Rig-Veda for a fresh point of view. From bráhman (nom. neut. *bráhma*, 'hymn or prayer') there is derived brahmán (nom. masc. *brahmâ*, the man of the bráhma, the hymnist or 'prāyer'). The brahmâ, as Muir[1] points out, was at first a poet or sage (= rishi, vipra, kavi, cf. RV., I, 80, 1), then a minister of public worship in general, and lastly a particular kind of priest with special duties. As the class of *Brahmâṇas* or Brahman-priests formed itself gradually, adherents thereto began to be designated in the later hymns and verses of the Rik by the names brahma-putrá (II, 43, 2, later addition, Grassmann) and especially *brâhmaṇá*, both meaning 'son of a Brahman-priest.'[2] When the distinction between Brahman and Kshatriya had been completely fixed, then as classes they were often designated by the abstract terms *Brahma* (Sacerdotium, Geistlichkeit, Priesthood) and *Kṣatram* (Nobility). Thus in the *White Yajur-Veda*, the *Atharva-Veda* and the *Brâhmaṇas* the two designations often stand side by side (*Brahma ca Kṣatram ca*). *E. g.*, *Vâj. Saṁh.*, VI, 3, VII, 21, XX, 25, XXX, 5; AV., II, 15, 4, XV, 10, 3; Çat. Br., III, 5, 2, 11. 'The Brahman and the Kshatra, these *two vital forces*.[3] So I, 2, 1, 7, IV, 2, 2, 13, IX, 4, 1, 7–11, etc. This meaning of bráhman, namely *priesthood*, seems to have been derived from both bráhman and brahmán.

There remains to be investigated only one more meaning of bráhman, but it is the greatest of all, namely Bráhman as the concept of the greatest energy, the highest reality, the self-existent. In the later hymns of the Rig-Veda we meet with Bráhmanaspáti (= Brihaspati) 'the Lord of prayer.' This is clearly a personification of the mighty power which lies at the heart of the bráhman or 'holy word,' and manifests itself in the wonder-

[1] OST., Vol. I, p. 243.

[2] Compare the O. T. name of a member of the class of *nebhîîm* 'prophets,' namely *ben-nâbhî* 'son of a prophet' (Amos, VII, 14).

[3] Cf. Plato's description of separate priestly and warrior castes, *Timaeus*, pp. 444, 445, Jowett's trans.

ful effects of the sacred formulas. It is to be noted that the appearance of Bráhmanaspáti coincides in general with the rise of the doctrine of the magical efficacy of the sacred texts. We have already studied the doctrine of bráhman *external and objective* as hymn, formula, and sacred text in general, and also the doctrine of bráhman *internal and subjective* as the sacred truth, wisdom, and theology of the holy word. *Bráhmanaspáti*, the apotheosis of the *power* of the holy word, introduces us to a third line of development. Very often in the *Brâhmaṇas* is Brihaspati identified with Bráhman, *e. g.*, Çat. Br., III, 1, 4, 15 '*Bráhma vai Bṛhaspati.*' So also III, 3, 1, 2, III, 7, 3, 13, III, 9, 1, 11–14, V, 1, 1, 11, V, 1, 4, 14, V, 3, 5, 7–8, IX, 2, 3, 3, etc. Compare also *Ait. Br.*, I, 19, 1, *Taitt. Saṁh.*, III, 1, 1, 4, etc. All this is significant. It indicates that for the theologians of the *Bráhmaṇa* period a deeper meaning was discovered in the word 'Bráhman' than had hitherto been found, to wit, the same meaning as had been expressed in the ancient hymns by Brihaspati, the personification of the *power* of the holy word. It will be sufficient for our purpose to illustrate this deeper meaning of Bráhman by suitable quotations from the literature of the period. Thus: *Taitt. Saṁh.*, VII, 3, 1, 4 'Limited are the Rik-verses, limited are the Sâma-verses, limited are the Yajus-verses, but there is no end to that which is *Bráhman*'; Çat. Br., III, 3, 4, 17 'The *Brahman* moves the gods onward'; IV, 1, 4, 10 'The *Bráhman* is the world-order (*ṛtam*)'; VI, 1, 1, 10 'The Bráhman is the *first born* (*prathamajam*) of this All'; VIII, 2, 1, 5 'The Bráhman is the highest of gods'; VIII, 4, 1, 3 'Heaven and earth are upheld by the *Bráhman*'; X, 3, 5, 10, 'This is the *Greatest Brahman* (*jyeṣṭham Bráhman*), for than this there is no thing greater'; X, 3, 5, 11 'This Bráhman has nothing before it and nothing after it,'; X, 4, 1, 9 'I praise what hath been and what will be, the *Great Brahman* (*mahad Bráhma*), the one *Akṣara*, the manifold Bráhman, the one *Akṣara*'; X, 6, 3, 1 'Let him meditate on the *True Brahman* (*satyam Bráhma*). Cf. II, 1, 4, 10 'The Bráhman is the truth (*satyam*)'; X, 6, 5, 9 'Bráhman is the Self-existent (*swayambhu*); reverence be to Bráhman!' Note also the following passages from the Atharva-Veda: X, 7,

24 'The gods, the knowers of Bráhman, meditate on the *Highest Bráhman*' (*jyeṣṭham Bráhma*, cf. Çat. Br., X, 3, 5, 10); X, 8, 1 'Reverence be only to that *Highest Bráhman*'; X, 7, 17 'The men who know the Bráhman know the *Highest* (*Parameṣṭhin*).' Thus Bráhman is not merely (1) the external *form* of the sacred word, and (2) the *meaning* of the sacred word, but it is also (3) the *power* which resides in the heart of the sacred word, and so in the heart of all things.

B. *Derivation of Bráhman.*

The word 'bráhman' is made up of *brah-* plus the common Indo-European suffix *-man.* This suffix forms *nomina actionis*, and more rarely *nomina agentis.* The *nomina actionis* vary between the meaning of the thing and the action. When used as infinitives (*e. g.*, *dā́-mane* = δό-μεναι) they indicate the action; when not so used, the thing. As examples cited by Brugmann[1] we have *mán-man* 'thought,' *vás-man* 'covering,' *dhâ-man* 'dwelling,' *dâ-man* 'gift,' *bhû-man* 'earth,' *bhár-man* 'support.' Or, to take a Latin example, *flu-men* 'river.' It is to be noted that the meaning in all these cases is concrete and not abstract. It is thought, raiment, house, gift, earth, support, and river, that the words mean, rather than thinking, dressing, dwelling, giving, being, supporting, and flowing. Brahman has two forms, *bráhman* and *brahmán*, which differ both in gender and in accent. They are used respectively as noun of action and noun of agent. With these we may compare *dhár-man* (n) 'support,' and *dharmán* (m) 'supporter'; also *dâ-man* (n) 'gift,' and *dâ-mán* (m) 'giver.' We know that in the case of *dharman* and *dâman* the roots are *dhar-* and *dâ-*. But brahman has exactly the same formation in every respect. We must therefore conclude that *brah-* in like manner represents a true root form. Professor Hopkins[2] with some hesitation connects Brahmán with "fla(g)men," and sees in it "an indication of the primitive fire-cult in antithesis to the soma-cult." There are two difficulties here. First the phonetic difficulty of connecting brah- with flag. The cognate

[1] *Comp. Gram.*, Vol. II, pp. 365–375.
[2] *Religions of India*, p. 168.

verbs Gr. *φλέγω*, Lat. *flagro*, Skt. *bhrâj*, and Germ. *blecken*, all seem to presuppose the IE. *bhleĝ*, while *bṛh* and *barz* go back to *bhṛĝh*. Again, this hypothesis has no support, so far as I can see, in the actual usage of brahman or of its cognates. Another equation suggested by Dr. Haug[1] in 1868, and lately championed by Wackernagel[2] is that Bráhman = Baresman, the bunch of sacred twigs used in the Zend ritual. If this be correct, then the root represented by *brah-* is *barh-(bṛh)* = Zend *barz*, from which *baresman* (= bares + man) is derived. Before this can be accepted, the change from *barh-* to *brah-* must be explained. Oldenberg[3] doubts such a change and remarks: "Baresman wäre vedisch *barhman; mit brahman hat es schwerlich etwas zu thun." But Wackernagel[4] shows pretty clearly that râ or ră sometimes stands in the place of âr or ăr not only before *ṣ* + consonant, but also before *h* + consonant, as in bráhman (*barh bṛh*) and *drahyánt* (*darh dṛh*). There is no doubt of the derivation of baresman from Zend *barz*, for, as Jackson[5] says, "Av. s sometimes results from Av. z becoming s before m;" and he cites as examples *maēsmana* 'with urine' (*miz* = *mih*) and *baresmana* 'with baresman' (*barz* = *barh*). We may take it as fairly well settled, then, that bráhman is the same word etymologically, both as regards root and suffix, as the Zend baresman.

The next problem is to determine the original meaning of the root *bṛh*. IE. *bhṛĝh* is postulated as the original of Skt. *bṛh* and Zend *barz*. There are many derivatives in Zend, *e. g.*, *barezant* (= *bṛhant*) 'high,' *barez*, *berez* 'high,' *barešnuš bareźâ* 'height,' *barezišta* 'very high' (Skt. *barhiṣṭha*). We have also in O, Ir, *bri* Gen. *breg* 'mountain,' *Brigit* 'the exalted' (Skt. *bṛhatî*, Zend *barezaiti*); in Armen. *berj* 'height'; in Gothic *baúrgs* 'fortress,' 'city' (cf. Germ. *Berg* and *Burg*); in Latin *fortis* (for *forgtus*) 'strong' (?); and in Sclavonic *brŭzŭ* 'quick' (?). Leaving out *fortis* and *brŭzŭ* as doubtful, we see that all the other cognates seem to have the meaning 'high,' being used primarily with

[1] *Ueber die ursprüngliche Bedeutung des Wortes Brahman.*

[2] *Altind. Gram.*, 1896, S. 213.

[3] *Veda*, S. 342, note 2.

[4] *Altind. Gram.*, S. 212, fg.

[5] *Avesta Grammar*, 1892, p. 51.

a spatial reference. The most important Skt. derivative from *bṛh-* is the participial form *bṛhat*, which occurs about 270 times in RV. As Grassmann points out, the word *bṛhat* very often stands side by side with certain adjectives denoting *extension* (*urú, pṛthú* 'broad,' *gabhîra* 'deep,' *ṛṣva* 'high') evidently as a general synonym. It very seldom goes with *mahát, mahi* 'great' (only three times). From the usage of *bṛhat* then the conjecture is plausible that the meaning of IE. *bhṛĝh* was 'to be extended' whether in length, breadth, depth or height. The most impressive form of extension is extension upward, and this is the meaning found in the Zend, O. Ir., and Gothic cognates. Let us test this conjecture as far as possible. The root *bṛh* (with the exception of the participle *bṛhat*) is used only transitively with prepositions and in the causative form without prepositions. It has only two fundamental meanings, 'extend,' and 'strengthen.' Unless there be some meaning still more concrete and fundamental underlying both, we must regard the meaning 'extend' as primary, and the meaning 'strengthen' secondary. That, as between these two meanings, the meaning 'extend' is primary is favored not only by the sense of the Zend, O. Ir. and Gothic cognates, but also by the fact that the meaning 'strengthen' can more easily be derived from 'extend' than vice versa. The connection between extending the hand and helping or strengthening another is well illustrated by the Arabic *madad* 'help,' lit. extension (of the hand). If in three passages of the RV. *bṛh* + *upa* or *sam* means apparently to press (as the arm upon or around some one), this meaning can be easily derived from *bṛh* in the sense of 'extend,' the transition in meaning being helped by the intensive form of the verb in two of the three cases. That the meaning of *bṛh* was 'to be extended' is further supported by the usage of *baṛhnā* and *baṛhānā* in the modern dialects of India, in which the meaning is almost if not quite exclusively 'extend.'

We are now prepared to consider the cognate words Baresman and Bráhman. We have seen that the root underlying both words means 'to be extended,' 'to be high,' and that the suffix *man* forms nouns of action. We should expect then that both baresman and bráhman, if used abstractly as infinitives, would have some such meaning as extending, exalting, presenting, offering; or, if not so used, then 'thing extended, lifted up, presented, offered.' How does the actual usage of baresman agree with this hypothetical sense? The word '*baresman*' is confined almost exclusively to the Yasna or sacrificial portion of the Avesta, where it occurs fifty or sixty times. As defined by De Harlez[1] it is a "faisceau de branches de tamarisque que le prêtre mazdéen doit tenir a la main, levé vers le ciel, pendant la récitation des prières." Thus baresman as a 'thing extended, lifted up, presented,' is the sacred bundle of twigs in the hands of the Mazdean priest. There is abundant evidence in the text of the Yasna that the uplifted Baresman in the hand of the priest was regarded as an emblem of adoration, prayer, and praise. Thus the following passages may be cited, as translated by Mills.[2] 'I desire to approach the stars, moon and sun *with the Baresman plants and with my praise*' (Yasna, II, 11); 'We present this plant of the Baresman, and the timely prayer for blessings' (XXIV, 3); 'This plant of the Baresman (and) the timely prayer' (XXIV, 8); 'We present . . . this branch for the Baresman, and the prayer for blessings' (Visparad, XI, 2). According to these passages the lifting up or presentation of the Baresman accompanied the recitation of the prayers and hymns of praise. That the Baresman or bunch of sacred twigs was an emblem of worship and adoration is supported by the similar use of palm branches among the Hebrews. Two passages may be cited. "After these things I saw and behold, a great multitude . . . standing before the throne and before the Lamb, arrayed in white robes *and palms in their hands*; and they cry with a great voice, saying, Salvation unto our God which sitteth on the throne, and unto the Lamb" (Apocal. Ioh., VII, 9–10). The scene is laid in the heavenly temple, where a great multitude of the redeemed as white-robed priests serve God day and night (v. 15) with palms in their hands and words of adoration on their lips. These are not palms of victory but palms of adoration. As held up or presented they are emblematic of worship just like Baresman.

[1] *Manuel*, p. 389. [2] SBE., Vol. XXXI.

Again in Evang. Ioh., XII, 12–13 we read: "A great multitude . . . took the branches of the palm trees, and went forth to meet him, and cried out, Hosanna: Blessed is he that cometh in the name of the Lord." We have also palm branches borne in the hand as emblems of salutation and praise. In fact the *uplifted* attitude has ever been one of the chief ways of expressing salutation and adoration. Consider the forms of modern salute. They are mostly variations of one fundamental attitude. In saluting one stands erect, or raises the hand, or presents arms, or lifts up the voice in a ringing cheer. Adoration is religious salutation. It is expressed in the Hebrew and Christian Scriptures by the uplifting of the person (Luke, XVIII, 11), or of the eyes (Ps., CXXIII, 1, Luke, XVIII, 13), or of the hands (Ps. LXIII, 4, 1 Tim. II, 8), or of the voice (Isa. XXIV, 14, 2 Chron., V, 13, Acts. IV, 24), or of palm branches borne in the hand (Apocal. Ioh., VII, 9; cf. 1 Mac. XIII., 51).

What then is the connection in meaning between Baresman and Bráhman? Both mean apparently 'thing extended, lifted up, presented, offered.' But in the Zend ritual 'the thing lifted up, presented, offered,' was the Baresman or bunch of sacred twigs, which like the palm branches of Apocal. Ioh., VIII, 9, was an emblem of worship, as it were a kind of *visible adoration.* While on the other hand in the Vedic ritual 'the thing lifted up, presented, offered,' was Bráhman, the 'hymn or prayer' of adoration, which like the lifting up of the voice in Isa. XXIV, 14, was also an emblem of worship, as it were a kind of *audible adoration.* As there is no essential difference betweeen an acted and visible, and a spoken and audible salute, so there is none, as regards original purpose, between *Baresman* acted and visible worship through the lifting up of the sacred branches, and *Bráhman* spoken and audible worship through the lifting up of one's voice in hymn and prayer.

For all this there is a striking analogy in Hebrew. The verb *rûm* means, like *bṛh* and *barz*, 'to be high.' In the Hiphil or causative it means 'to lift up,' both of an offering as presented, and of the voice as raised in prayer and adoration. These two uses of *hêrîm* are represented by the two derivatives *terûmâh* and *rômâm.*

The former means offering as something lifted up or presented in the ritual, and is rendered 'heave offering.'[1] The latter[2] means a lifting up of the voice in adoration, an offering of 'the fruit of the lips,' and is rendered in the Revised Version 'high praise,' and by Canon Cheyne, 'lofty hymn.'[3] Terûmâh, 'heave offering' is the analogue of Baresman; *rômâm*, 'lofty hymn,' the analogue of Bráhman.

There is no essential difference between 'lifting up the voice in prayer' and 'lifting up a prayer.' Both idioms occur, the first in Isa. XXIV, 14, Acts IV, 24 and the second in Isa. XXXVII, 4, Jer. VII, 16. In fact the word *vâc* (Lat. *vox*) in the RV. has the double meaning 'voice' and 'hymn or prayer.' In actual usage bráhman is a synonym of *vâc*. Both derivation and Vedic usage would be expressed if we should render 'lofty hymn.'

Before the separation of the Persian and Indian branches of the Aryan people, Baresman and Brahman were one word and so had a common meaning. That meaning has already been referred to from the point of view of etymology as 'thing extended, lifted up, presented, *offered*.' Combining etymology with usage, we get '*religious offering*' in general as the most probable meaning of *Baresman-Brahman* in the prehistoric period. The diverse meanings of Baresman, 'the offering of sacred branches,' and Brahman, 'the offering of hymn and prayer,' may be regarded as differentiations of the original meaning of 'religious offering' in general. Another hypothesis is possible, to wit: that the offering of sacred branches accompanied by hymn and prayer, as described in the Avesta, was the original meaning of Baresman-Brahman, and that while Baresman has maintained its meaning unchanged, Brahman has undergone a transference of meaning, the custom of offering sacred branches having dropped out of use among the Indians, and so Brahman being applied exclusively to the remaining element in the ritual, namely the offering of hymn and prayer. The first hypothesis seems to me to be the safer one. Centuries intervened between the prehistoric period

[1] Cf. Ex. XXIX, 27, 'The thigh of the heave offering . . . which is heaved up.'
[2] Pss. LXVI, 17, CXLIX, 6. Text unfortunately not absolutely sure.
[3] *The Book of Psalms*, N. Y., 1895.

when Baresman and Brahman were one word with one meaning and the period of religious practice reflected in the earliest Indian and Persian sources. It is quite possible that in the prehistoric period Baresman-Brahman may have referred to the 'lifting up' or 'offering' of many things, *e. g.*, the parts of the animal sacrifice (cf. Heb. terûmâh), sacred branches, sacred formulæ of hymn and prayer, etc.

The dominant explanation of the word 'bráhman' is that of Professor Roth (St. Petersburg Lexicon) who makes it to mean originally "die als Drang und Fülle des Gemüths auftretende und den Göttern zustrebende Andacht." He is followed by Whitney,[1] who says that bráhman is "from the root *barh* 'exert, strain, extend,' and denotes simply 'worship' as the offering which the elevated affections and strained desires of the devout bring to the gods"; and also by Deussen,[2] who defines the original meaning of bráhman as "der zum Heiligen, Göttlichen emporstrebende Wille des Menschen." According to this explanation, bráhman is not *the uplifted voice* of the priestly worshiper in prayer and hymn so much as *the uplifted soul*,[3] the exaltation of the spirit in worship. Both ideas undoubtedly involve each other to some extent. The question is which is the more primitive idea. It seems to me that the weight of the evidence is in favor of the more concrete notion as being the more primitive. In the Vedic period religion was ritualistic, cosmological, objective. It is only when we reach the period of the Upanishads that religion becomes psychological and introspective, in a word, subjective. In the course of the Upanishad speculations Bráhman undoubtedly came to mean something not altogether different from the "Wille" of Schopenhauer. But to hold that this was the original meaning of bráhman seems to me a violent anacronism. The following considerations may be adduced against this theory: (1) Out of 240 or more passages in which the word 'bráhman' occurs in the RV. Grassmann finds the meaning "Erhebung des Gemüthes" in only five. But in these

[1] *Or. & Ling. Stud.*, 1873, p. 28, note.
[2] *Vedânta*, S. 128.
[3] Cf., Ps. XXV, 1.

passages also bráhman can be interpreted without violence as 'hymn or prayer.' The phrase *brahmanâ vandamâna imâm dhiyam* (III, 18, 3 only here) alone gives any support to the view of Grassmann. But it may be rendered 'through a hymn (*bráhman*) uttering this meditation' as well as by 'through inward devotion (*bráhman*) uttering this hymn.' (2) To assign to bráhman as its fundamental meaning 'the exaltation of the spirit in worship' illustrates the psychological danger, in connection with the interpretation of all ancient texts, of reading them in the light of modern ideas. For, as Professor Max Mueller says,[1] "Though the idea of prayer as swelling or exalted thought may be true with us, there is little, if any, trace of such thoughts in the Veda." (3) The interpretation of *Sâyaṇa* the great orthodox commentator on the Rig-Veda (d. 1387 A. D.) is worth noticing. He halts between the meanings 'hymn' (*mantra, stotra*) and offering (*yajña, anna*). But if our interpretation is correct, bráhman in the RV. is nothing else than just a hymn lifted up, presented, *offered* to God in worship. According to this, *Sâyaṇa* is not so very far wrong after all.

To go back to the original meaning of *bṛh* (*bhṛĝh*), it is possible, as already hinted, that it was more concrete than either 'extend' or 'strengthen.' The meaning 'grow' would fit in very well. That which grows extends itself and becomes strong. To make to grow is to 'make big and large.'[2] But if 'grow' was the original meaning of *bṛh*, it was dropped at a very remote period, and only the derived meanings 'extend' and 'strengthen' retained. So far as I am aware, *bṛh* is never used in the sense of either 'to grow' or 'to make to grow' (of something organic). Still the meaning 'to grow' is assumed by the Dhâtupâth (*vṛddhau*) and accepted by Haug, Max Mueller, *et al.* There is no objection to the hypothesis that the prehistoric meaning of *bṛh* was 'to grow,' provided that it be remembered that this meaning was early dropped, and so cannot be supported by actual usage in the historic period. For *barz*, Jackson[3] gives the meanings

[1] *Six Systems of Indian Philosophy*, p. 70.
[2] Whitney, *Roots*, 1885.
[3] *Avesta Gram.*, p. 51.

'*grow up*, be high, great.' The Zend derivatives all apparently mean 'high' or 'height' alone, with the possible exception of Baresman, which, as meaning bunch of twigs, may contain a hint of an original meaning 'to grow up,' therefore growth.

C. *Connection of the various meanings of Bráhman.*

Having finished the discussion of the derivation and usage of bráhman, we are prepared to consider the problem of the unification of its various meanings. These are, as given by Roth: (1) pious utterance in divine worship, (2) holy formula, (3) holy word, (4) holy wisdom, (5) holy life (the Brahmanical *chastity*), (6) the Absolute, (7) holy order (the Brahmanical *community*). Of these meanings nos. (5) and (7) must be eliminated as of complex derivation. The meaning 'chastity' (no. 5) is clearly derived mediately through the idea of *brahmacarya*, the life of the brahmacârin or theological student, of whom strict chastity was required. And the meaning 'holy order' or 'priesthood,' as already pointed out, is to be derived from the joint idea of bráhman and brahmán. Perhaps, too, bráhman came to be used in the sense of 'priesthood' as the correlative of *Kṣatra* 'nobility' (cf. *Bráhma ca Kṣatram ca*), *i. e.*, through the working of the principle of analogy. There remain, then, five meanings of bráhman to be unified. We begin with the Vedic meaning as 'hymn or prayer.' How bráhman came to have this meaning has been sufficiently indicated. We are not justified in assuming that brahman had first the meaning of 'word' in general, which only afterwards received the specialized sense of religious or sacred word. Historically, we have to begin with the meaning 'hymn or prayer.' There is no direct proof of any meaning more primitive in Sanskrit. Bráhman, as 'hymn or prayer,' gradually with the creation of a sacred literature came to have the larger meaning of 'holy word' in general. This process may be illustrated from the parallel process in the Old Testament. Here the most primitive unit of revelation is the *tôrâh* or oral deliverance of the priest on some matter pretaining to religious life or worship. But since the first canon was a collection ot such *tôrôth* or 'laws,' the word *Tôrâh* came to have a more comprehensive sense as the *Tôrâh* or 'Law' (of Moses). Finally the meaning of *Tôrâh* was so enlarged that it covered the whole Old Testament in its antithesis to the New (cf. Evang. Ioh., I, 17). The use of the word 'Veda' is analogous. It may mean either (1) the Rig-Veda, or (2) all three (or four) Vedas, or (3) the whole religious literature known as *Çruti* or Revelation in its antithesis to *Smriti* or Tradition.

It has already been pointed out that the five remaining meanings of bráhman may be reduced easily and naturally to three: namely (1) Bráhman, the *objective* word as sacred hymn, sacred formula, and sacred text in general; (2) Bráhman, the *subjective* word as sacred wisdom and theology, the content and meaning of the objective word; and (3) Bráhman *the Immanent Word*, the energy which manifests itself in both sacred hymn and sacred order, and indeed in all things. In this way the various meanings of Bráhman are articulated together in one common organism and so unified. There is indeed a development of meaning, but it is both natural, and, in a sense, inevitable. For consider the parallel development in the West. In the O. T. we have the three stages fairly well represented: (1) The *Tôrôth* or deliverances of the priests concerning matters of worship. These when finally collected formed the objective word. (2) The *Debhar-Jahweh*, or message of Jahweh through the prophet, in which there was a larger emphasis on the *inner* content or doctrine of the word; and (3) the Hochmâh *Wisdom*, of Jahweh, which in Prov. VIII, is hypostasized. In Greek philosophy, too, especially in Stoicism, we have (1) λόγος ενδιάθετος, 'the internal word,' (2) λόγος προφορικός, 'the external word,' and (3) λόγος σπερματικός, 'the *immanent* word' or reason of God, which works in the heart of all things. These two streams, namely Hebrew religion and Greek philosophy, find their synthesis in the New Testament: and so we have there also a threefold doctrine of the word as: (1) Scripture, the written and objective word; (2) the inner meaning and content of the word as 'truth' (Evang. Ioh., XVII, 17), 'spirit and life' (Id. VI, 63); and (3) the Λόγος as the Divine, Heavenly and Creative Word. May we not say in words used by Oldenberg in another connection that this dialectic movement in Hebrew, Indian, Greek, and Christian thought "has something of the calm inevitable necessity of a natural process?"[1]

It is no wonder that some scholars have sought to provide a basis for the meaning 'word' as the original meaning of bráhman by trying to connect *bṛh* with *vṛdh* 'to grow,' from which *verbum, Wort, word,* may perhaps be derived. The attempt can hardly be pronounced successful. There seems to be no possible phonetic connection between *bhṛĝh* and *vṛdh;* and besides even the connection of verbum, etc., with *vṛdh* is disputed.[2] Moreover, the attempt is unnecessary. Bráhman gets the meaning 'word' in its own way. As a name for Vedic 'hymn or prayer' it came gradually in the course of the growth of the Indian doctrine of Holy Scripture, to mean 'the holy word.' The threefold development of meaning, as explained above, is not at all dependent on the question of derivation. Any one of the synonymous terms for 'hymn' or 'prayer,' as *e.g., stotra* or *manîṣâ,* might have had the same development, if *stotâras* or *manîṣiṇas* had acquired the supreme position which the Brahman-priests acquired. I here submit a (tentative) synopsis of the meanings of the word bráhman. Its derivatives, *Brahmán, Bráhmanaspáti,* and *brahmacarya,* must be introduced in order to make the synopsis complete.

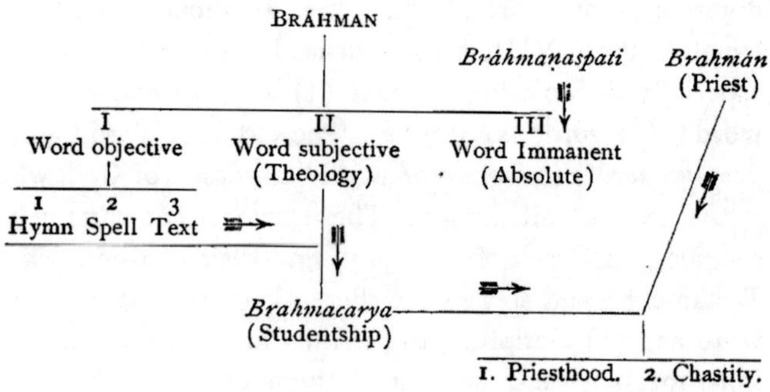

[1] *Buddha,* p. 29.

[2] *E. g.,* by Meyer (*Griech. Gram.,* 1896, S. 231, 320), who connects *verbum* with Gr. εἴρω √Ϝερ 'to say' *i. e., ver-bum.*

CHAPTER II.

The Development of the Doctrine of Unity in the Pre-Upanishad Literature.

A.

The growth of the monistic conception in the period of the Rig-Veda and in the region of the Panjâb.

Deussen remarks that "the first and oldest philosophy of a people is to be found in their religion."[1] This is preëminently true of the religion of the Rig-Veda, because of the speculative element which was present from the very beginning. The oldest hymns reveal a naïve childlike conception of nature as displayed in its most striking manifestations. The sun in the heavens, the fire on the hearth, at once beneficent and destructive, the storm-winds, the thunder-bolt, the blushing dawn, the all-embracing heaven—these were the things which called into activity the religious and speculative tendencies of the Vedic Aryans. Take the case of fire (*agni*). Professor Max Mueller has written the biography of Agni,[2] in which the theogonic process is manifest by which agni 'fire' becomes finally Agni 'god.' The principle of causality seems to have been at work together with the primitive tendency to personification. We have, then, personification, idealization and apotheosis as processes connecting agni 'fire' with Agni 'god.' Or, to put it in another way, Agni, the mystery of fire, seemed to demand for its explanation an agent or genius. Hence behind agni-phenomenal was postulated, as *we* would say, agni-noumenal, the genius of fire, who was idealized and elevated to divine honors. Thus natural law was conceived anthropomorphically. In the search after causes 'the gods were the first philosophy.'[3]

A gradual change or movement is discernible in Vedic thought. Since the gods were 'an intellectual creation'[4] of the Aryan

[1] *Geschichte*, S. 77.
[2] *Physical Religion*, pp. 144–176.
[3] Max Mueller, *Six Systems*, p. 48.
[4] Deussen, *op. cit.*, S. 79.

mind, the same power which made could also unmake. Hence successive deities rise above the horizon as it were, have their period of ascendancy and then decline. Thus, in the age of the Rig-Veda Dyâus and Varuna are vanishing gods. Indra, the warrior god, holds the supreme place in the Vedic pantheon, the greatest number of hymns being written in his honor. But even Indra is finally doubted and ridiculed.[1] Prajâpati is just mentioned in the Rig-Veda, but in the period of the Yagur-Veda he is, like Zeus, 'the father of gods and men.' Some of the later Vedic gods are mere products of speculative abstraction. Thus *Bráhmaṇaspáti* is simply the hypostasis of the power of the bráhman 'hymn or prayer'; *Prajâpati*, of the power of generation, and *Tapas* of the power of austerity.

Further, the movement discernible in the conception of deity is, on the whole, a movement towards a doctrine of unity. Such a tendency was involved in the Vedic conception of nature. As Oldenberg says: "Für den vedischen Glauben ist die ganze den Menschen umgebende Welt beseelt."[2] This being so, then sooner or later speculative thought was bound to grasp the one underlying 'self' or 'soul' of things. We may compare early Greek philosophy, in which a hylozoistic conception of nature soon reached its logical conclusion in the monism of the Eleatic school. Again, the use of *deva*, 'the bright heavenly one,' as a general epithet of the gods, seems to carry with it the suggestion at least that all the gods participate in one common nature or essence. At any rate there is evidence of a tendency toward classification and fusion, all of which points in the direction of unity. Thus, according to their spheres of activity, the gods receive a threefold classification as gods of the sky, gods of the mid-air, and gods of the earth. The number of the gods was apparently constructed on the basis of this threefold division, since they all represent multiples of three, as three or thirty-three or thirty-three million. Further, on the basis of unity of *function* we have the conception of 'dual gods,' *e. g.*, Indra-Varuna, Indra-Soma, Agni-Soma, Indra-Agni, etc., according to which two

[1] Cf. RV, II, 12, 5, VIII, 100, 3, X, 119, etc.
[2] *Veda*, S. 39.

gods are combined in the dual and then viewed as a unity. Sometimes, too, the functions of all the gods are apparently conceived as overlapping and more or less identical, and so there is the name Viçve Devâs, 'all-gods,' which name is easily interchangeable with any abstract designation of the divine totality. All of this betrays the first crude beginnings of a systematizing and unifying spirit. Closely related to the tendency to syncretism and fusion, is another parallel but perfectly distinct tendency, which Max Mueller has aptly called *Henotheism.* This term describes the impulse of the Vedic poet to withdraw his attention from all other devas and to exalt for the time being the immediate object of adoration, whichever deva it may be, into a supreme deity. As Eggeling says: "It is this *immediateness of impulse* under which the human mind in its infancy strives to give utterance to its emotions that imparts to many of its outpourings the ring of monotheistic fervor."[1] Henotheism may be regarded as a kind of dim recognition of an underlying unity. As Schroeder says: "Es ist eine Tendenz, die uns zuletzt hinführt zu der Erkenntniss dass all die verschiedenen Göttergestalten im Grunde gar nicht von einander unterschieden sind, dass sie alle im Grunde doch nur Einer sind, dass aus dem Einen sie alle sich entfaltet, eine Tendenz zum Glauben an das ἓν καὶ πᾶν, zum *Pantheismus.*"[2] For we must bear in mind that the Vedic gods are rarely if ever thought of quite apart from the natural forces and phenomena of which they are in most cases mere personifications. As such they might easily be thought of as only various manifestations of the One Reality, the mystery that dwells in all things. So, *e. g.*, in the hymn of Dîrghatamas (I, 164, 46):

> That which is *one* the sages call diversely;
> They name it Agni, Yama, Mâtariçvan.

And so when Agni, for example, is approached by the devout singer, he may be conceived, as *we* would say, not simply as a manifestation of the One Reality, but rather as the One Reality itself under a special manifestation.

[1] *Ency. Brit.*, IX Ed., Art. Brahmanism.
[2] *Kultur*, S. 76.

To illustrate this conception of the underlying unity of things, as it is set forth in the Rig-Veda, I have selected for special treatment the seven hymns which from this point of view seem to me most important. These are hymns 72, 81, 90, 121, 125, 129 and 190 of the tenth book. Of these I offer the following metrical translations. The aim is simply to reproduce the thought and meter of the original, and I, of course, make no claim to literary excellence. The order is after Deussen.

The Hymn of Creation, X, 129.

1. Then was there neither being nor non-being,
Nor airy sphere nor heaven overarching;
What covered all? and where? in whose protection?
Was there a sea, a deep abyss of waters?

2. Then was nor death nor anything immortal,
No night was there, nor of the day appearance.
Breathed breathless then in self-existence *That One*,
Other than it, of any kind, there was not.

3. Darkness there was; and by the darkness covered
Was all this world at first, a wat'ry chaos;
A germ lay hidden in its secret casing,
Which by the might of heat was born as *That One*.

4. From whom in the beginning love developed,
Which is the primal germ of conscious spirit;
The bond of being in non-being seeking
Poets with insight in the heart discovered.

5. Across all things their measuring-line extended.
What was above, and what was found beneath it?
Seed-bearers were there and developed forces;
Beneath, self-power; above, its revelation.

6. But who knows, who is able to declare it,
Whence sprang originally this creation?
Afterwards came the gods into existence;
Who then can know from whence it had its being?

7. How this creation came into existence,
Whether as uncreated or created;
He who in highest heaven looks out upon it,
He knows forsooth, or does not even he know?

The Hymn to Hiraṇyagarbha, X, 121.

1. In the beginning rose *Hiranyagarbha*,
Born as the single lord of every creature ;
He, too, it was that stablished earth and heaven,—
What god shall we adore with sacrifices ?

2. He who gives breath and strength, and whose instruction
Revered is by the gods and all the creatures ;
Whose shadow immortality and death is,—
What god shall we adore with sacrifices ?

3. He who in majesty is the one monarch
O'er all things breathing and o'er all things dying,
Who rules two-footed and four-footed creatures,—
What god shall we adore with sacrifices ?

4. He by whose might exist these snowy mountains,
The ocean and the stream of which they fable ;
Whose all-embracing arms are the world-regions,—
What god shall we adore with sacrifices ?

5. He through whom sky is firm and earth is steady,
Through whom sun's light and heaven's arch are stablished ;
Who fixed the airy sphere twixt earth and heaven,—
What god shall we adore with sacrifices ?

6. He to whom look the rival hosts in battle,
Sustained by his support and anxious-hearted ;
O'er whom he as the sun new risen shines forth,—
What god shall we adore with sacrifices ?

7. When first the mighty all-pervading waters
Came germ-containing, agni-generating,
Thence rose he who is of the gods the *one life*,—
What god shall we adore with sacrifices ?

8. E'en he who in his might surveyed the waters,
Which force contain and sacrifice engender ;
Who o'er the gods rules as the one supreme god,—
What god shall we adore with sacrifices ?

9. May he not harm us, he, earth's generator,
He who with order fixed begat the heaven,
And gendered, too, the bright and mighty waters,—
What god shall we adore with sacrifices ?

10. Prajâpati, than thee there is no other,
Who holds in his embrace the whole creation;
May that be ours which we desire when off'ring
Worship to thee, may we be lords of riches.

The Hymn to Tapas and Samvatsara, X, 190.

1. From Tapas, the all-glowing heat,
Were generated law and truth;
From it was generated night,
And from it, too, the swelling sea.

2. And from the ocean's swelling tide
Begotten was the circling year;
Which ordereth the day and night,
And ruleth all that move the eye;

3. Which, as creator, stablished well
In order fair the sun and moon,
The heavens also and the earth,
The atmosphere and light of sun.

The Hymn to Viçvakarman, X, 81.

1. He who has entered, off'ring, into all things,
As the wise sacrificer and our father;
He through the prayer of men desiring riches,
Through all the lower world diffused his being.

2. But what served as a standing place . . .
What as a firm-set basis and in what way,
From which earth-generating Viçvakarman
With might o'erarched the heavens, seeing all things?

3. On all sides are his eyes, his mouth on all sides,
On all sides are his arms, his feet on all sides.
The *one god* he with mighty arms and pinions
Forges together heaven and earth, creating.

4. What was the forest, what indeed was that tree,
From which the gods have hewn out earth and heaven?
Ye sages wise, search out in spirit this whereon
He took his stand, when he established all things firm.

5. What are the highest mansions and the lowest,
And these here in the midst, O Viçvakarman,
That teach thy friends! And, O thou self-existent,
Strong one, in off'ring offer up thine own self.

6. Strengthened by sacrifice, O Viçvakarman,
Do thou thyself offer up earth and heaven;
And though on all sides men in error wander,
May he be our rich lord of sacrifices.

7. Him now, who quick as thought is, let us summon,
Lord of speech Viçvakarman, for our succour.
May he delight himself in all our service,
Who blesseth all and doeth good to all men.

The Hymn to Bráhmaṇaspáti, X, 72.

1. The genesis of the bright gods
We will declare with wonder deep,
Uttered in hymns for him who shall
In coming generations hear.

2. Bráhmanaspáti like a smith
Together forged whatever is;
When gods existed not as yet,
Then being from non-being rose.

3. In times when gods existed not,
Then being from non-being rose,
The spaces of the world were born,
From her they call Uttânapad.

4. The earth was from Uttânapad
Born, and the spaces from the earth;
From Aditi arose Daksha,
Again from Daksha Aditi.

5. Born first of all is Aditi,
Who, Daksha, thine own daughter is;
After her were the gods produced,
The blessed and immortal ones.

6. When ye stood in the swelling flood,
Ye gods, who well established are;
Then as from dancers from you whirled
Upward in mighty clouds the dust.

7. When ye like mighty athletes caused
The worlds, ye gods, to emanate,
Then lifted ye the sun on high,
That in the ocean hidden lay.

8. Eight valiant sons had Aditi,
Who from her body were produced.
With seven she went among the gods,
While she the egg-born cast away.

9. With seven sons went Aditi
Up to the ancient race divine;
The egg-born she surrendered to
The sway of birth and now of death.

The Hymn to Vâc, X, 125.

1. I wander with the Rudras and the Vasus
With the Âdityās and the Viçve Devas;
'Tis I that cherish Varuna and Mitra,
Indra and Agni and the heavenly horsemen.

2. The soma-plant streaming with juice support I,
Tvashtar and Pûshan I support and Bhaga.
'Tis I that give wealth to the sacrificer,
Who offers zealously the pressed out soma.

3. I am the queen, the gatherer of riches,
The knowing, first of those that merit worship.
Me have the gods in every place established,
That omnipresent I may enter all things.

4. Through me it is that mankind breathe and eat food,
See what is visible and hear what's spoken.
In me unconsciously they have their being;
Hear one and all, my word deserveth credence.

5. Whoever speaks, 'tis I that am the speaker,
Uttering things pleasing both to gods and mortals.
Whom I delight in, powerful I make him,
Make him a Brâhman, or a sage or Rishi.

6. I too am he that bends the bow for Rudra,
That his keen shaft may smite the Brahman-hater.
'Tis I that stir men with the joy of battle,
Both earth and heaven I fill with mine own essence.

7. In highest heaven bore I the heaven-father,
Yet is my birthplace in the ocean-waters;
From thence divided am I into all things,
And with my height reach up to yonder heaven.

8. 'Tis I that wind resemble as it blows hence;
Thus do I reach and comprehend what e'er is
Beyond sky yonder and beyond this earth here;
So great have I become through mine own greatness.

The Hymn to Purusha, X, 90.

1. A thousand heads has Purusha
A thousand eyes, a thousand feet;
The earth surrounding on all sides,
He reached beyond ten fingers' length.

2. All this vast world is Purusha,
Both what has been, and what will be;
He ruleth all who deathless are
Through the all-potent sacrifice.

3. As great as this is Purusha,
Yet greater still his greatness is;
One-fourth of him is all this world,
Three-fourths th' immortal in the heaven.

4. Three-fourths ascended up on high,
The other fourth developed here;
He spread himself o'er all that is,
What lives by food and what does not.

5. From Purusha was born Virâj,
And from Virâj too Purusha.
As soon as Purusha was born,
He reached beyond earth everywhere.

6. With Purusha as off'ring when
The gods prepared a sacrifice,
Spring was the sacrificial grease,
Summer the fire-wood, Autumn drink.

7. The gods as off'ring on the straw
Sprinkled the first-born Purusha;
With him the gods made sacrifice,
The Rishis and the Sâdhayas.

8. From him as whole burnt offering
Dripped off the sacrificial fat;
Therefrom were made fowls of the air,
And animals both wild and tame.

9. From him as whole burnt offering
Rik-verses rose and Sâma-hymns;
The poems, too, were born of him,
Of him the sacrificial songs.

10. Horses sprang from him and all beasts
Which have on both jaws cutting teeth;
Of him the cattle were produced,
Of him were born both goats and sheep.

11. When they dismembered Purusha,
In what ways was he then transformed?
What did his mouth and arms become?
And what his thighs and his two feet?

12. His mouth became the *Brâhmaṇa*,
And his two arms the *Kṣatriya;*
His thighs became the *Vaiçya-class*,
From his two feet the *Çûdra* came.

13. The moon was gendered from his mind,
And from his eye the sun was born;
Indra and Agni from his mouth,
And from his breath the wind was born.

14. Born of his navel was the air;
The sky was from his head brought forth,
Earth from his feet, and from his ear
The quarters; so the worlds were made.

15. Seven sticks confined the altar-fire,
Thrice seven sticks as fuel served;
The gods prepared the sacrifice,
And bound as victim Purusha.

---

16. With sacrifice the gods made sacrifices,
These sacred usages were thus primeval;
The gods, the mighty ones, attained to heaven,
Which they of old inhabit as the Sâdhyas.

The contents of these hymns, so far as they are of philosophic import, may be summarized as follows :

(1) Philosophy with the Vedic Aryans as with the Greeks was born as 'the child of wonder.' Questions emerged. What was the origin of things (X, 129, 6)? What existed in the beginning (X, 129, 1)? What was the material out of which the world was made (X, 81, 4)? What was the standing-place of creation (X, 81, 2)? Was the world created or not (X, 129, 7)? Who is the God who is worthy of sacrifice (X, 129, 2–9)? When these questions were asked, there was no separation between philosophy, the search for natural causes, and theology, the doctrine of the gods, for the gods as deified natural forces fell within the sphere of nature. Thus the Vedic thinkers were concerned at once with the origin of the gods (*devânâm jânam*, X, 72, 1) after the manner of the Theogony of Hesiod, and with the origin of things (*jâtavidyâ*, X, 71, 11) after the manner of the early Ionic School. In other words, the philosophy of the Rig-Veda was a cosmology described in terms partly mythological and partly philosophical. The following points of contact with Greek Philosophy may be noticed in passing. The place of *Kâma* 'love' in the Creation-hymn (X, 129, 4) reminds us of ἔρως in the Theogony (v. 120) of Hesiod. The use of *vana* 'forest' and *vṛkṣa* 'tree' with reference to matter as the building material of the universe (X, 81, 4) is exactly the same as that of the Greek ὕλη. The conception, too, of the original element as water (vid. X, 125, 7; 72, 6–7; 121, 7–9; 190, 2; 129, 1, 3) reminds one of the theory of Thales and also of the similar view of the Hebrews.[1] Aditi, 'the free,' 'the boundless,' 'the infinite,' as a name for the primeval matter (X, 72, 4–5) is not unlike the ἄπειρον of Anaximander. The most interesting parallel, however, is between the Indian *sat* and *asat*, on the one hand, and the Greek τὸ ὄν and τὸ μή ὄν on the other. The neuter participle *sat*, from *as* to be, is etymologically the same as ὄν. In these Vedic hymns, there is no absolute antithesis between being and non-being as there is with the Eleatics and with Plato; for being is said to be born of non-being (X, 72, 2–3) and the bond or root

[1] Cf. Amos VII, 4, Ex. XX, 4, Gen. I, 2, Ps. XXIV, 2.

of being is discovered in non-being (X, 129, 4). The theory implied is not unlike the dynamic view of Aristotle, according to which non-being or matter is the promise and potentiality of being or form.[1]

(2) The origin of the world[2] was conceived in three ways: as a process of architecture, as a process of generation, and as a process of sacrificial dismemberment. These different conceptions, especially the second and third, are often combined in the same hymn. The notion of the world-process as a process of building, underlies the names Tvashtar, 'the carpenter god,' Viçvakarman, 'the all-worker,' and Dhâtar and Vidhâtar, 'the ordainer,' 'the creator.' It also underlies the question (X, 81, 4) from what material (*vana, vṛkṣa,* ὕλη) the world conceived as a house to be built was hewn. Closely connected with this is the conception of the world as the work of a creative smith who forges or welds together heaven and earth (X, 81, 3; 72, 2). In these representations we have the germs of the 'design' argument in its crudest form. But the dominant conception of the world-process is as a process of generation. Thus whatever is (*sat*, X, 72, 3) is born, including heaven and earth (X, 121, 9), sun and moon (X, 90, 13), the four Vedas (X, 90, 9), law and truth (X, 190, 1), the animals (X, 90, 10), the gods (X, 72, 1, 5), original matter conceived as the infinite (X, 72, 4, Aditi = ἄπειρον) and as the primeval watery chaos (X, 121, 9; 190, 1; 90, 5), nay, the One Reality itself in its empirical development as *Tad ekam* 'that one' (X, 90, 3), *Hiranyagarbha* 'the golden germ' (X, 121, 1), *Samvatsara* 'the creative year' (X, 190, 2), *Daksha*, 'creative force' (X, 72, 4), *Vâc*, 'the creative word' (X, 125, 7), and *Purusha*, 'the cosmic man' (X, 90, 5). The third conception of creation as a process of sacrificial dismemberment is found especially in two hymns. In the first, namely, X, 81, Viçvakarman, the apotheosis of the energy of nature, is represented as a sacrificial priest (hotar, v, 1) who in creating the world continually offers up earth and heaven (v, 6), *i. e.*, his own

[1] Such points of contact are not evidences of borrowing. They belong rather to the category of 'developmental coincidences.'

[2] Cf. Wallis, *Cosmology of the Rig-Veda*, p. 89.

body (v, 5) as the totality of things. This conception is expressed still more clearly in X, 90, where Purusha, 'the cosmic man,' is represented as dismembered and offered up by the devas (personified forces of nature), from which sacrificial dismemberment all things derive their being.[1] Closely related to this is the view of creation as the result of *Tapas* 'heat,' 'austerity,' 'creative fervour' (X, 129, 3; 190, 1). As Deussen remarks: "Tapas und Opfer, diese beiden höchsten Bethätigungen menschlicher Kraft, haben ihr Vorbild in dem Verhalten Gottes bei der Weltschöpfung."[2] All three views of the creative process were suggested by experience. The Vedic Aryans built houses of wood; they begat children; and they dismembered animals in sacrifice. And so they conceived creation after the analogy of architecture, generation and sacrificial dismemberment.

(3) An original primciple self-existent, unitary and all-comprehensive was postulated (Tad Ekam, 'that one,' X, 129, 2; Purusha, 'the cosmic man,' X, 90, and Daksha, 'creative force,' X, 72, 4). From this original principle was produced the chaos of matter[3] conceived as *aditi* 'the infinite' or as *salilam, âpas, virâj*, 'the primeval waters.'[4] Then as the third step in the process, the first principle itself underwent an empirical development and was born of the matter which had been produced by itself. This explains the paradoxical statements:

> 'From Aditi arose Daksha
> Again from Daksha Aditi,
> Born first of all is Aditi,
> Who, Daksha, thine own daughter is' (X, 72, 4-5).

And again,

> 'From Purusha was born Virâj,
> And from Virâj too Purusha' (X, 90, 5).

Thus there were three moments in the drama of creation: (*a*)

[1] The source of this conception is clearly to be found in the creative efficacy which was gradually imputed to the sacrifice.

[2] *Geschichte*, S. 136.

[3] Cf. Hesiod *Theogony*, v, 115.

[4] Compare the three parallel terms in Gen. I, 2, viz., *tôhû wâ bhôhû, tehôm and hammayim.*

the Original Being (transcendent), (*b*) the world of chaotic, indiscrete matter, the primeval abyss, and (*c*) the Original Being (phenomenal) as the First-born and Ruler of all things.[1]

(4) Let us glance briefly at the place and functions which now remain to the devas. They are not banished, neither do they lose their personification entirely. They are simply brought into a relation of subordination to the One Reality as effects of the One Cause (X, 129, 6; 125, 1–2; 90, 13), as individual forces of the one all-Comprehensive Force (X, 125, 3; 90, 6–7; 72, 6), as sharers in the One Life (X, 121, 7), and as obedient subjects (X, 121, 2, 8; 90, 2) and ministers (X, 72, 7; 81, 4) of the One Lord. In their capacity as subjects and ministers of a Supreme Lord the devas are not unlike the *malachîm* 'angels' of the Old Testament.[2]

(5) Thus the tendency of the later Vedic hymns is toward unity, but this unity is described sometimes in the terms of monotheism and sometimes in the terms of monism. The One Reality when conceived monotheistically is called *Eka Deva* 'the One God' (X, 81, 3; 121, 8), *Eka Pati* 'the One Lord' (X, 121, 1) and *Eka Râjâ* 'the One King' (X, 121, 3). These epithets have a Semitic ring. They remind us of the Hebrew Psalms, in which God, Lord, and King are frequent names of Deity. The characters essential to a consistent monotheism are the unity, the personality, the sovereignty, the transcendence and the holiness (= righteousness) of God. The first three seem to be found in the *Hiraṇyagarbha-Prajâpati* hymn (X, 121); and the fourth, possibly in the monistic hymn to *Purusha* (X, 90), according to which only one-fourth of Purusha was converted into phenomenal existence, while the other three-fourths remained, as originally, "immortal in the heaven" (v. 3). For the idea of the holiness of God we have to go back to the august and commanding figure of Varuna (cf. V, 85), "the King of all" (v. 1), who awakens in his worshippers the consciousness of sin (vv. 7–8); who upholds moral order (*ṛtam*) and punishes its breach. Thus we have in the Rig-Veda the scattered germs of an ethical mono-

[1] Vid. Deussen, *Op. cit.*, S. 57.

[2] Cf. Ps. CIV, 4: 'Who maketh his angels winds, his ministers a flaming fire.'

theism. In two ways such a monotheism might have been realized. A single Aryan tribe or community through the teaching of Rishis, having the ethical earnestness of Hebrew prophets, might have maintained and developed the ethical conception of Varuna, and so outstripped all the rest in zeal for righteousness. Hence there might have arisen a rivalry between Varuna and the Devas, just as between Jahweh and the Baalim, with final victory for Varuna. This, as we know from Hebrew history, would have been a practical mode of genesis for an ethical system. How far this was from accomplishment in the period of the Rig-Veda is manifest from the words of Deussen, himself an ardent admirer of things Indian, to the effect that the ethical element, in which the real worth of a religion lies, falls in the Rig-Veda surprisingly into the shade.[1] Or, again, a new god (like Prajâpati, the lord of all creatures) might have been discovered in answer to the question 'What God shall we adore with sacrifice?' and then conceived as 'the One God above the gods,' the older devas or gods being degraded to the position of 'ministering angels.' Such a movement towards monotheism is actually disclosed in the Prajâpati-hymn. It represents the highest reach of the Vedic striving towards monotheism.

But the dominant trend of Vedic thought was towards a monistic conception of things. Even where, as in the Prajâpati-hymn, One God is mentioned as above all gods, we are not absolutely certain that it is anything more than a nominal monotheism. The *Eka Deva* may be only a theological name for the totality of nature like the '*Deus*' of Spinoza. According to the monistic conception of things the one reality was viewed most consistently as neuter and impersonal, Tad Ekam, τὸ ἕν, 'that one' (X, 129, 2). But it also bore other names, which are less impersonal, such as *Purusha* (X, 90).

(6) It is to be noted finally that *Brahmaṇaspati*, the apotheosis of the power of the bráhman 'hymn or prayer,' and *Vâc*, the apotheosis of speech as incarnate in the Vedic words, are both made to refer to the ultimate reality. Vâc declares her own greatness (X, 125) quite in the manner in which *Sophia* (*Hoch-*

[1] *Op. cit.*, S. 82.

mâh, Prov. VIII) declares hers. *Vâc*, like *Brahmaṇaspati* and *Purusha*, is an anticipation of the later Bráhman, the One Reality, just as *Hochmâh* 'the Divine Wisdom' is an anticipation of the *Logos* of the New Testament.

B.

The growth of the monistic conception in the period of the Yajur-Veda and in the region of Madhyadeça.

Each of the four Vedas, when used in the wider sense, has three portions: (*a*) the *Saṁhitâ* or collection of hymns, (*b*) the *Brâhmaṇa* or collection of 'priestly discourses,' which explain the practical use of the hymns in connection with the various sacrifices, and (*c*) the *Sûtra*, a brief and systematic exposition of the content of the *Brâhmaṇa* after the manner of a modern catechism. Further, each *Brâhmaṇa* as a rule contains three subdivisions: (*a*) the *Brâhmaṇa* in the narrow sense, consisting largely of ceremonial prescriptions, (*b*) the *Âraṇyaka* or 'forest-treatise' at the end of a *Brâhmaṇa*, in which the sacrificial cult is spiritualized, and (*c*) the *Upaniṣad* or 'mystic doctrine' at the end of the *Âraṇyaka*. These divisions may be illustrated from the famous *Çatapatha Brâhmaṇa*, which contains fourteen books, of which the first thirteen make up the *Brâhmaṇa* in the narrow sense, and the fourteenth the *Âraṇyaka*, while the last six chapters of the fourteenth book compose the *Upaniṣad* known as the *Bṛhadâraṇyaka Upaniṣad*. There is another analysis of the contents of a *Brâhmaṇa*, as given by Madhusûdana Sarasvati, the author of the *Prasthâna-Bheda*,[1] into *vidhi*, 'prescription,' *arthavâda* 'exposition,' exegetical, mythological, dogmatical, etc., and lastly *Vedânta* 'the end of the Veda,' both as conclusion of the Veda, since the *Upaniṣads* represent the final stages of Vedic literature, and as *aim* of the Veda, since the *Upaniṣads* contain the philosophy of the Vedas.[2] The period of the *Yajur-Veda* (also called the *Brâhmaṇa* period) I understand to include whatever literature

[1] Vid. Deussen, *Geschichte*, S. 47–50.

[2] With the ambiguity of the word Vedânta we may compare the similar ambiguity in the use of the Metaphysics (τὰ μετὰ τὰ φυσικά) of Aristotle, as following the Physics both in order and in theme.

falls between the *Rig-Veda Saṁhitâ* and the *Upaniṣads, i. e.*, the *Yajur-Veda Saṁhitâ*, the *Atharva-Veda Saṁhitâ* and the *Brâhmaṇas* in the narrow sense.

First to be noticed is the cleft between the period of the hymns of the *Rig-Veda*, and the time of the composition of the oldest *Brâhmaṇas*. When the curtain of history rises for the first time in India, we see the Aryans (probably in the second millennium, B. C.) tending their flocks, fighting their battles, and singing their hymns in the land of the five rivers. The great monument of this period is the *Rig-Veda Saṁhitâ*. Then there follows a period of obscurity, of migration and conflict. The centre of Aryan life and thought shifts from the Panjâb to the Madhyadeça, the region of the upper Ganges and Jamna. The great monument of the second period, which I have called the period of the *Yajur-Veda*, is the *Brâhmaṇa* literature. In this period the hymn-collections of the *Yajur-Veda* and *Atharva-Veda* were made and probably the canon of the *Rig-Veda Saṁhitâ* was not closed before this time. The *Brâhmaṇas* as a literature may be briefly characterized. They represent the earliest Indo-European prose. They pre-suppose the Vedic hymns. As ritualistic theological and philosophical appendices to the Vedic hymns they bear a relation to them similar to that borne by the Talmudical literature to the Old Testament. The *Brâhmaṇas* are, as it were, a bridge between the Vedic hymns and the *Upaniṣads*. We see in them symbolism gone mad. Everything is equated with everything else. They illustrate the fact that ritualism thrives on symbolism. Deussen warns us against taking their (apparently) philosophical ideas too seriously.[1] The warning is needed. Still the wild and incoherent identifications of the *Brâhmaṇas* indicate, at least, the trend and general direction of Indian speculation.

Let us now address ourselves to the philosophy of the period, especially as revealed in the pages of the *Çatapatha Brâhmaṇa;* for, as Oldenberg says, " In none of the Vedic texts can we trace the genesis of the conception of the unity in all that is, from the first dim indications of this thought until it attains a steady bril-

[1] *Op. cit.*, S. 174.

liancy, as clearly as in that work, which next to the hymns of the Rig-Veda, deserves to be regarded as the most significant in the whole range of Vedic literature, the '*Brâhmaṇa of the hundred paths.*'"[1] Here two things are important for our purpose, first, to see how far the philosophical ideas already discovered in the *Rig-Veda Saṁhitâ* suffer modification or development, and secondly, to summarize the steps in the genesis of the meaning of Brahman as the One Reality.

Prajâpati, who just emerges above the horizon in the *Rig-Veda Saṁhitâ* is in the zenith of his power in the *Brâhmaṇas.* To illustrate at once the mania for identification which characterizes the *Brâhmaṇas*, and the nature of Prajapati "the great God" (*mahân Deva*, Çat. Br., VI, 1, 3, 16) of this period, I submit the following list of identifications from the Çat. Br. Prajâpati is declared to be the sacrifice (I, 5, 2, 17), the year (I, 2, 5, 12), everything (I, 3, 5, 10), speech (*vâc*, I, 6, 3, 27), the *brahmán* of the gods (I, 7, 4, 21), the earth (II, 1, 4, 13), Agni (II, 3, 3, 18), mind (IV, 1, 1, 22), truth (IV, 2, 1, 26), the self (*âtman*) (IV, 6, 1, 1), heaven and earth (V, 1, 5, 26), father and mother (Id.), soma (Id.), the great god (VI, 1, 3, 16), *Hiraṇyagarbha* (VI, 2, 2, 5), *Ka* (Id.), the worlds and the quarters (VI, 3, 1, 11), the whole *bráhman* (VII, 3, 1, 42), and *Viçvakarman* (IX, 4, 1, 12). I think we can detect a certain method in this madness of identification. Prajâpati, as the lord of generation and becoming, the apotheosis of nature, is clearly a mythological name for the totality of things viewed as the One Reality. And so Prajâpati may be identified with 'everything' in general after the manner of Purusha (RV., X, 90, 2), or with various individual things of fundamental cosmic import already mentioned in the RV., such as sacrifice (cf. RV., X, 90, 15), the year (*Samvatsara*, cf. RV., X, 190, 2); speech (*vâc*, RV., X, 125), the Great God (cf. the *Eka Deva* of RV., X, 121), *Hiraṇyagarbha* and *Ka* (RV., X, 121), and *Viçvakarman* (RV., X, 81). Other identifications such as 'heaven and earth,' 'father and mother,' etc., simply indicate Prajâpati's character as the substance and support of all things. The identification of Prajâpati with *Âtman* (Çat. Br., IV, 6, 1, 1) and with the

[1] *Buddha*, p. 25.

whole *Bráhman* (VII, 3, 1, 42) is indicative of the growing influence of what finally became the *Brahman-Âtman* doctrine of the *Upaniṣads*. The cosmic character of Prajâpati must not be overlooked. He is especially identified with the year (Samvatsara), the ever-recurring cycle of the birth and decay of nature. For a similar representation on the part of a Christian poet, compare the lines in Thomson's Hymn to the Seasons:

> "These as they change, Almighty Father, these
> Are but the varied God; the rolling year
> Is full of Thee."

As the Creative Year Father Prajâpati loses his strength through much production and so is relaxed (in winter). He therefore has to be renewed through sacrifice which the gods (especially Agni, the returning fire and heat of Spring) offer through the renewed activity of the forces of nature. Hence Prajâpati is at once the father and the son of Agni, the father and the son of the devas. Prajâpati is the original principle. He alone was here (or all this) in the beginning. Çat. Br., II, 2, 4, 1; II, 5, 1, 1; VI, 1, 3, 1. His primal impulse is desire of offspring.[1] Tapas ('austerity,' 'creative fervour') and sacrifice are the creative means. He himself is at once sacrificial priest (through the devas his own forces) and sacrificial victim. Thus he produces all things, *devas* and *asuras* (the bright and dark forces of nature), *Brahman*, *Kṣatra* and *Viç*, yea all living creatures. He is both the "defined and the undefined, the limited and the unlimited."

From all this it is clear that there is no great advance as yet beyond the incipient philosophical doctrine of the Vedic hymns. What we find is simply a change of emphasis. The Vedic *Hiraṇyagarbha*, *Viçvakarman*, *Vâc*, *Samvatsara*, *Puruṣa*, are all mentioned, but they fall far behind Prajâpati in importance. They, so to speak, lose their being in his, and find it again only through identification with him. Prajâpati is enriched with the attributes of all of them and so appears as the one supreme being. Nor is the doctrine of the gods essentially different from

[1] Cf. RV., X, 129, 4.

what we have found in the philosophical hymns of the Rig-Veda. As regards their cosmic character, the devas are viewed as the members and senses of the all-embracing world-man (Çat. Br., III, 2, 2, 13; VII, 1, 2, 7). Varuna, as the lord of law (*dharmapati*, V, 3, 3, 9), is still the holy god. Whoso commits adultery sins against Varuna (II, 5, 2, 20) and falls into his "noose." The mysticism of the *Brâhmaṇas* is justified by the oft-repeated declaration that "the gods love the mystic." There are "two kinds of gods," divine and human. "The gods, forsooth are the gods; and the learned Brâhmans versed in sacred lore are the human gods" (IV, 3, 4, 4). Coming now to the doctrine of sacrifice, we notice that it has at once a cosmic and a human character. The sacrificial activity of the priests finds its antitype and justification in the sacrificial activity of the gods. As in the philosophical hymns of the Rig-Veda, so here also the world-process is viewed as an eternal sacrifice, of which the one all-embracing reality (Prajâpati, X, 2, 2, 1, Purusha, III, 5, 3, 1, and later Bráhman, XIII, 7, 1, 1) is the victim. *Yajña* 'sacrifice' is a kind of apotheosis of the eternal process of becoming after the manner of the doctrine of Heraclitus. Gods, men, and *pitris*, all exist because of the sacrifice. The gods obtained their position and authority through sacrifice. Through it, too, men are delivered from "Varuna's noose." Hence the sacrifice is "the most excellent work" (I, 7, 1, 5), "the great inspirer of devotion" (III, 5, 3, 12), a thing in its real nature "invisible" (III, 1, 3, 25), "the self (*âtman*) of the gods" (VIII, 6, 1, 10). The doctrine of the all-sufficiency of the sacrifice reached its climax in the *Brâhmaṇas*.

A word or two may be added with reference to the doctrine, in this period, of a primeval matter. It does not differ essentially from that which we have already found in the Rig-Veda. Thus in the *Taitt. Saṁh.* (V, 6, 4, 2 and VII, 1, 5, 1) we read that "water forsooth was here (or all this) in the beginning, a chaotic mass,"[1] and that "Prajâpati as wind[2] moved upon it." In Çat. Br., XI, 1, 6, 1, there is also a mention of the primeval watery chaos, from which Prajâpati is said to have sprung,

[1] *Salilam*, cf. RV., X, 129, 3. [2] *Vâyu*, cf. *rûah*, Gen. I, 2.

Deussen sees in this last passage an attempt to dethrone Prajâpati by allowing him only a relative and phenomenal existence. In VI, 1, 1 we have a further description of the primeval matter as non-being[1] in the words: "In the beginning non-being was here (or all this)."

So much then with reference to the philosophico-religious ideas of the *Brâhmàṇas* in their relation to the kindred ideas of the Vedic hymns. It only remains now to summarize briefly the steps in the genesis of the meaning of Bráhman as the One Reality. The contribution of the Vedic hymns to the genesis of this meaning consists (*a*) in the development of the notion of the power and efficacy of Bráhman 'the sacrificial formula,' and (*b*) in the apotheosis of this notion under the name of *Bráhmaṇaspáti*. In the period of the *Brâhmaṇas*, Bráhman, as already pointed out, has the meanings: (*a*) Word objective, as hymn, formula, text, (*b*) word subjective, as sacred wisdom and theology and (*c*) word immanent, as both the power which energizes in the world and the world as the manifestation of such power. The third meaning of Bráhman came naturally, since Bráhman finally took the place of Purusha and Prajâpati and so fell heir to their connotation.

The transition from meanings (*a*) and (*b*) to meaning (*c*) may be illustrated by means of several passages from the *Çatapatha Brâhmaṇa*. In VI, 1, 1, 8–10 Prajâpati is represented as creating first of all Bráhman, the Triple Science (*i. e.*, the three Vedas *Rik*, *Sâma* and *Yajus*, viewed as one doctrine). This became a foundation for further creative activity. Next from Vâc (= Bráhman, Veda) as a standing place he created the waters, into which finally along with the Triple Science he entered as the world-egg. From this again Bráhman was produced empirically as the first-born of this all. This is but a development of ideas already found in the Rig-Veda, especially X, 129. A similar conception is found in the oft repeated words of VII, 4, 1, 14, *Brahma jajñânam prathamam purastât*, 'The Bráhman first born in front,' according to which Bráhman is described under the figure of the sun, which is born day by day in the east. Thus far Prajâpati and Bráhman have

[1] *Asat*, cf. RV., X, 129, 1, 4.

stood more or less on a level. Bráhman has even been described as dependent upon Prajâpati. But in the later books of the Çat. Br. Prajâpati decreases and Bráhman increases. This gradual growth of Bráhman into the supreme principle is indicated by such texts as VIII, 4, 1, 3, 'The Brahman is the highest of gods'—'Heaven and earth are upheld by the Bráhman'; X, 3, 5, 10 'This is the greatest Bráhman'—'This Brahman has nothing before it and nothing after it'; XI, 2, 3, 1 'Brahman forsooth was this world in the beginning.' These passages bring us finally to the highest conception of Bráhman as *Svayambhu*, the Self-Existent (X, 6, 5, 9; XIII, 7, 1, 1), where we reach the position of the Upanishads.

The exaltation of Bráhman as the one immanent and all-embracing reality suggests the question, not why the word 'brahman' received this meaning, but why after having once received it, the meaning has always been retained. There have been other names for the ultimate reality, *e. g.*, in the Rig-Veda *Puruṣa*, *Vâc*, *Prajâpati*, and in the Atharva-Veda *Kâla* 'Time,' *Skambha* 'support,' *Prâṇa* 'spirit,' etc. These have emerged at different times, but have always been superseded, or at least remained secondary. Bráhman, however, has endured as the supreme name of the Ultimate Reality. Why? It seems to me that there is no other answer except this that the word 'Bráhman' is also the name of the collective Brâhman community, and so Bráhman, as the name of the Ultimate Reality, had the powerful support of the priesthood. The word *Bráhman*, like *Brahmán*, *Bráhma-Veda* and *Brâhmaṇa*, fell within that potent circle of words and ideas on which hang in large measure the civilization and thought of India.

CHAPTER III.

THE DOCTRINE OF BRÁHMAN IN THE UPANISHADS.

A. Remarks on the Sources.

The word '*upaniṣad*' requires explanation. It is used in the sense of 'mystic import,' 'secret name,' 'hidden sense,' 'secret doctrine.' For example, Çat. Br., X, 5, 1, 1,[1] 'The mystic import of the fire-altar doubtless is speech.' Thus far there is no difference of opinion. The derivation of the actual meaning from the word '*upaniṣad*,' however, is not so clear. Most modern scholars, *e. g.*, Roth,[2] Weber,[3] Mueller,[4] explain '*upaniṣad*' as meaning originally the sitting at the feet of a teacher (*upa-ni-sad*) therefore 'session,' 'séance,' 'Sitzung.' But, as Professor Max Mueller says,[5] no passage has yet been found in which the word '*upaniṣad*' is used in the sense of 'session' or in the sense of pupils approaching and listening to their teacher. Oldenberg[6] takes *upaniṣad* as a synomyn of *upâsanâ* 'Verehrung,' comparing *upa-âs* with *upa-niṣad*. The reasoning is suggestive but not conclusive. The earliest as well as most important passage bearing on the meaning of *upaniṣad* is Çat. Br., IX, 4, 3, 3. 'He thus makes the common people below subject (*upaniṣâdin*) to the nobility.' On the basis of this passage Hopkins[7] suggests that the original reference of the word '*upaniṣad*' was to "subsidiary works of the ritualistic *Brâhmaṇas*." This conjecture suggests another, which seems to me to be better supported by actual usage, namely, that *upaniṣad* had the meaning of secondary sense, as opposed to primary sense. It is true that the crucial passage for the original meaning of *upaniṣad*, as cited above, does not

[1] As translated by Eggeling.

[2] *Skt. Wörterbuch*, St. Petersburg.

[3] *Indische Literaturgesch.*, Berlin, 1876, S. 30.

[4] *Three Lectures on the Vedânta Philosophy*, p. 23.

[5] SBE., Vol. I, pp. lxxx–lxxxi.

[6] ZDMG., 1896, Bd. 50, S. 457 ff.

[7] *Religions of India*, pp. 217, 218.

in itself decide the question. The meaning of *upaniṣâdin* 'subsidiary,' 'subject,' 'secondary,' suggests for the word '*upaniṣad*' a reference either to the attitude of pupils sitting at the feet of a teacher, or to literary works subsidiary and supplementary to other works, or again to meanings subsidary and secondary to other meanings. The first reference cannot be supported by any quotations, and the second is relatively late. The third alone is supported by actual usage in the earliest Upanishads. Thus in the earliest passages in which the word '*upaniṣad*' occurs, namely, at the end of the *Çâṇḍilya* and *Yâjñavalkya* portions respectively of the Çat. Br., the word refers to unusual interpretations of sacrificial and ritualistic details. The *yajus* or sacrificial formula (X, 3, 5, 12), the fire-altar (X, 5, 1, 1) and the year (XII, 2, 2, 23) had each of them its own *upaniṣad*, *i. e.*, 'esoteric meaning' or 'mystery.'[1] This seems to be the most primitive meaning of '*upaniṣad*.' But an esoteric meaning, an allegorical interpretation, is distinctly subsidiary and secondary to the primary and natural sense. I would therefore take the original meaning of *upaniṣad* to be neither 'session,' nor 'subsidiary works of the ritualistic *Brâhmaṇas*,' but rather the secondary and allegorical as opposed to the primary and natural sense. It is a meaning found in a word because put there by speculative insight. If we take *upaniṣad* to be 'supplementary sense' after the analogy of *upâkhyânam*, 'supplementary tale,' then *upaniṣad* might be explained etymologically as the mystic sense which resides in (*ni-sad*) a word in addition to (*upa*) the primary sense. Such a meaning, although secondary as opposed to the natural sense, is by no means secondary as regards importance. In the earliest passage in which, so far as I know, the word '*upaniṣad*' occurs, namely, in the *Çâṇḍilya* portion of the Çat. Br. (X, 3, 5, 12), we read that the 'mystic import is the essence of this *Yajus*,' *i. e.*, the important thing in a sacrificial formula is the allegorical and mystical sense, not the primary sense. All this is in harmony with the maxim of the *Brâhmaṇa* period that 'the gods love the mysterious.'

But allegory and mysticism are not confined to the Upani-

[1] Cf. Apocal. Ioh., I, 20, 'the mystery of the seven stars.'

shads, but are common to the *Brâhmaṇas* also. Why then is the term '*upaniṣad*' restricted in its application? For one thing it is a comparatively late word, appearing for the first time in what are properly the Upanishad-portions of the Çat. Br. Then, too the word '*upaniṣad*' seems to have been from the very beginning confined to mystical speculations of a definite kind, namely those pertaining to the investigation of Bráhman. Thus the earliest mention of *upaniṣad* (Çat. Br., X, 3, 5, 12) occurs in the same context where Bráhman is described (vv. 10, 11) as the 'greatest' (knowledge or reality), than which 'there is nothing greater.' And in Kena Up. 32 we have the expression *Brahmî Upaniṣad* 'the mystic doctrine of Bráhman.' Thus *upaniṣad* came to be the standing term for theological as opposed to sacrificial mysticism. The Indian interpretation of *upaniṣad* as the destruction of ignorance through the knowledge of Bráhman may not be so far wrong after all.

Allegory has ever furnished an apparently easy way of uniting heterogeneous worlds of thought. Philo Judæus used it as a means of harmonizing Mosaism and Platonism; and in recent times it has been employed by Pandit Dayânanda Saraswati, founder of the Arya Samâj, as a means of discovering in the Vedas the science of the present day. What then more natural than that men who had been born and bred in the atmosphere of Indian ritual should seek to transcend the standpoint of ritualism by trying to discover a deeper meaning in the ritual itself. In other words, the mystics of the *Brâhmaṇa* period, like the author of the Epistle to the Hebrews, saw in the sacrificial ritualism a system of types and symbols, by means of which as a ladder they sought to climb up into the sphere of eternal realities.

The usage of the word '*upaniṣad*' has undergone a certain development. It means first of all secret name, secret sense, secret doctrine, *rahasyam*, μυστήριον, and in this sense is found in the oldest parts of the oldest Upanishads (Brih., II, 1, 20, Chând., I, 1, 10, I, 13, 4, Kaush., II, 1, Taitt., I, 3, 1, Ait. Âr., III, 1, 1, 1, III, 2, 5, 1). It means, secondly, verse or section containing the doctrine of Bráhman (Taitt., II, 9, 1, III, 10, 6, Chânḍ., I, 13, 4, III, 11, 2–3); and, thirdly, a collection of such doctrines in the form of a dogmatic text-book belonging to a particular school or sect.

The number of such dogmatic text-books is large. Professor Weber's list[1] contains 235. Some of these, however, may be duplicates. They belong to different periods of time. Three ways of classifying the Upanishads may be mentioned. First, on the basis of their use by Çankarâcârya, the great Vedântic commentator, they fall into two classes: (*a*) orthodox or classical Upanishads, which furnish the proof texts for Vedântism, and (*b*) sectarian Upanishads, of which only a few are quoted. The classical Upanishads are eleven or twelve in number, and have been translated by Professor Max Mueller.[2] Secondly, on the basis of the different Vedic schools, we may distinguish between the Upanishads of the first three Vedas, which are eleven in number and almost entirely orthodox, and the Upanishads of the Atharva-Veda, which, with a few exceptions, are sectarian, heterodox, and relatively late. Thirdly, on the basis of the development of thought in the different Upanishads, we may rightly, I think, make the following classifications: First, *tentative* Upanishads, five in number, namely, *Bṛhadâraṇyaka*, *Chândogya*, *Aitareya*, *Kauṣîtaki* and *Taittirîya*.[3] These occupy the first place, both in age and in importance. The argument for their age is cumulative. They are integral parts of the great *Brâhmaṇas*, and their style is the old *Brâhmaṇa* prose style. They present numerous illustrations of the allegorical interpretation of the ritual. Each Upanishad is a collection of upanishads in the primary sense of the word. Their method is not dogmatic, but tentative and inquisitive. Their authors appear as "seekers after truth" and their thoughts have rightly been styled "guesses at truth." The dialogue and the parable are frequently employed as literary forms.

Of these five Upanishads the largest and also the most important are the *Bṛhadâraṇyaka* and the *Chândogya*. Çankarâcârya, in his great work on the Vedânta-Sutras makes about 2000

[1] *Literaturgeschichte*, S. 171, note.
[2] SBE., Vols. I, XV.
[3] Cf. Deussen, *Sechzig Upanishads*, S. 264.

quotations from the Upanishads. Of these fully two-thirds are from the *Chândogya* and the *Bṛhadâraṇyaka*.[1] The second class may be denominated the *dogmatic* Upanishads and includes in general the rest of the pure Vedânta Upanishads, especially *Îsâ*, *Kaṭha*, *Muṇḍaka*, *Çvetâçvatara*, and the poetic sections of *Kena*, *Bṛhadâraṇyaka* (IV, 4, 8–21) and *Mahânârâyaṇa*.[2] Here the thought is more mature and positive, and is set forth by preference in a poetical dress. The poetic sections are in general nosegays of Vedântic sayings bound together without much regard to inner connection. Innovations appear. Although the ideas are in general in harmony with those of the five oldest Upanishads, yet here and there may be detected the germs of other types of doctrine, especially of the *Sâṁkhya* and *Yoga* and of the great sectarian systems. The second class of Upanishads is clearly more developed than the first. Still later in point of development than the Upanishads of the second class are those of the third class, which may well be called the sectarian Upanishads, since they are simply the dogmatic text-books of a transformed and sectarian Brahmanism. Of the third class of Upanishads, Deussen has translated no less than forty in his masterly volume, *Sechzig Upanishads des Veda*. Among these sectarian Upanishads might well be reckoned the *Bhagavadgîtâ*, since it has a distinctly sectarian character and is also called an Upanishad. To sum up, then, the Upanishads really fall into two great groups, which may be roughly described as (1) the group of Upanishads of the first three Vedas = the classic Upanishads used by Çankarâcârya = (*a*) tentative and (*b*) dogmatic Upanishads, and (2) the group of Atharva-Veda Upanishads, which are in general sectarian, heterodox and late. The first great group represents the creative period of Indian philosophy, which may with some degree of confidence be assigned to the period 800–300 B. C. The second great group belongs in the main to the literature of the Hindu Revival, and so falls somewhere within the period covered by the last two thousand years.

[1] Vid. Deussen, *Vedânta*, S. 32 ff. for statistics.

[2] After Deussen. Cf. also A. A. Macdonell, *A History of Sanskrit Literature*, 1900, p. 226.

B. Doctrine.

We notice a gradual change in the point of view from which the doctrine of unity is treated. Thus, as already indicated, the standpoint of the pre-Upanishad literature may in general be characterized as cosmological—the standpoint of common sense. The unity described is a concrete and all-comprehensive unity. The world is conceived as a colossal man (Purusha, RV., X, 90). This symbol suggests an organic view of the universe as a system of interrelated forces and processes, the home of life and development. All this of course is expressed in a very naïve and poetic form. In the Upanishads, on the other hand, there is an attempt to transcend the common-sense point of view. The world of experience is no longer regarded as the thing-in-itself. Speculative thought probes beneath the surface of things in its quest for reality. This attitude was not without anticipations even in the Vedic hymns. Especially in the hymn to *Vâc* (X. 125) is there the conception of an *immanent Word*, something like the Stoic λόγος σπερματικός, a force which dwells and operates in all things, and in which unconsciously all men have their being.

The great theme of the Upanishads is *the quest for reality.* This is beautifully expressed in three Yajus-verses quoted in *Bṛhadâraṇyaka Upanishad*, I, 3, 27:

> "Lead me from the unreal to the real!
> Lead me from darkness to light!
> Lead me from death to immortality!"[1]

Different degrees of reality are recognized. Thus, we read in Chând. Up., I, 1, 2: "The essence of all beings is the earth, the essence of the earth is water, the essence of water the plants, the essence of plants man, the essence of man speech, the essence of speech the Rig-Veda, the essence of the Rig-Veda the Sâma-Veda, the essence of the Sâma-Veda the Udgîtha." This re-

[1] In the matter of quotations from the Upanishads it is difficult accurately to express my obligation to different scholars. I commonly follow Prof. Max Mueller's translation (SBE., Vols. I and XV), but not infrequently I modify it by Professor Deussen's renderings. I also make independent translations at times.

gressus from earth, the coarsest essence of things, back step by step to the *Udgîtha*, the supreme formula of the Sâma ritual, and, as represented by its introductory syllable *Om*, the symbol of the ultimate reality, illustrates at once a peculiarity of the style of the older Upanishads and the mystical interpretation of the ritual which characterizes them. Another instance of such a regressus from the conditioned to the unconditioned is found in *Bṛh. Up.*, III, 6, where the world of experience is represented as "woven like warp and woof" in the worlds of water, the worlds of water in the worlds of the sky, the worlds of the sky in the worlds of the Gandharvas, and so on successively through the worlds of the sun, of the moon, of the stars, of the Devas, of Indra, of Prajâpati, until finally "the worlds of Bráhman" are reached, beyond which inquiry cannot be made. Again, in several passages (*Kauṣ.*, II, 14, *Bṛh.*, I, 3, *Chând.*, I, 2, V, 1) there is mention of a controversy among the different *prâṇas* (breaths, senses, vital powers) as to which is the greatest. The controversy is always settled in favor of 'the breath in the mouth' (*mukhya prâṇa, âsanya prâṇa*), because breathing endures when all the other life-powers (hearing, seeing, etc.) are quiescent in sleep or destroyed. But although the *prâṇas* or vital activities have a certain reality (and 'the breath in the mouth' more than all the rest), yet there is something more real than these. The *prâṇas* are 'real' (*satyam*) and also their correlatives 'name' and 'form' (*Bṛh. Up.*, I, 6, 3), but the Âtman (ego or self) which underlies them is 'the real of the real.'[1]

One more instance of the search for reality may be given, and it is the most impressive of all, namely the famous *Koçavidyâ* or 'doctrine of involucra' in Taitt. Up., II. It begins with a statement of the order of creation, here a progressus from the Âtman. Thus "from that Self sprang ether, from ether wind, from wind fire, from fire water, from water earth, from earth plants, from plants food, from food seed, from seed man." Having such a genesis, man must be very complex. He is derived ultimately from the Atman.[2] What part of him is identical with

[1] *Satyasya satyam Bṛh. Up.*, II, 1, 20.

[2] Cf. Luke III, 36 "Which was the son of Adam, which was the son of God."

his source? What is the real man, the real self? It is not 'the man made out of the essence of food' (*annarasamaya*), the physical man, as we would say, for this aspect of man's nature may be stripped off like an outer husk. Nor is it the vital self consisting of breath or life (*prâṇamaya*), for this too may be eliminated. So with the self consisting of thought and will (*manomaya*), and the self consisting of cognition and worship (*vijñânamaya*). They do not represent the real self, and so may be stripped off. Finally, the core of reality both in man and in nature is found in the self consisting of bliss (*Ânandamaya*), the inmost self of all. This reality of realities is defined psychologically as 'the ear of the ear, the mind of the mind, the speech of speech, the breath of breath and the eye of the eye' (*Kena.*, I, 2, *Bṛh.*, IV, 4, 18), yea as 'the light of lights' (*Bṛh.*, IV, 3, 6, IV, 4, 18), compared with which the light of sun, moon and fire is only secondary. From these different instances, we see that when thought is cosmological, the search for reality is either *backward* toward the 'one only without a second'[1] from whom the whole world-process begins, or *upward* to the world of Bráhman which comprehends all worlds; but when thought is psychological, it is a movement *inward* toward the Ego or Self. As already remarked, there is as yet no sharp distinction between the real and the unreal. Realty presents itself as a thing of degrees. Still we notice a growing difference in the use of the old Vedic *sat* and *asat*, 'being' and 'non-being.' In harmony with the cosmological point of view, *sat* in the Rig-Veda means the world of natural objects as it presents itself to the ordinary understanding, the world of experience as we would say; while *asat* 'non-being' refers to that primitive undifferentiated condition of things which the early philosophers of both Greece and India postulated as the antecedent of the present ordered world. This point of view is still maintained in Taitt., II, 7, where *sat*, the world distinguished by 'name and form' is said to be born of *asat* 'non-being.' But in Taitt., II, 6, there emerges the first germ of the distinction between the world as empirically real but transcendentally unreal, and Bráhman as empirically unreal but

[1] *Chând. Up.*, VI, 2, 1 cf. Gen., I, 1, John, I, 1.

transcendentally real. Thus the cosmological Bráhman as the ordered world of experience is described as the sphere of being (*sat*), definition, relation, consciousness, and reality (*satyam*); while, on the other hand, Bráhman as the empirically unknown ground of all reality is characterized as transcendent, undefined, absolute, unconscious, and (empirically) unreal. The next step is to make explicit the doctrine that the true Bráhman is transcendentally real (*sat*), and this is done in a passage which well deserves to be called the monistic Confession of faith, namely: 'In the beginning there was only Being (*sat, τὸ ὄν*) *one only without a second*' (Chând. Up., VI, 2, 1). This is naturally accompanied by a polemic against the position still entertained in Taitt., II, 7, and Chând., III, 19, 1: 'In the beginning there was non-being.' 'How,' said Uddâlaka, 'could that which is be born of that which is not?' This is the standpoint of the later formulas: *Etad vai tad*, 'This (as described) is that,' (*Kaṭh. Up.*, 12 times), and *Om! tat sat*, 'That is real.'

Tat tvam asi, 'That art thou,' so reads the supreme identification of the Upanishads. In the light of what has gone before, this cannot mean, as sometimes interpreted, that man in his totality is equated with God. It can only mean that the core of reality in man, *i. e.*, his inmost self, is divine. This is not essentially different from the O. T. doctrine, that man is made in the image of God[1] or from the N. T. doctrine that man (Adam generic) is the son of God.[2] As President Schurman says: "I am unable to see how we can believe in God without at the same time regarding the finite spirit, as far as its essential ground is concerned, as identical, within the limits of its range, with the infinite spirit. It is so because it is an ego."[3] This participation in, or identity with the divine nature, it may be noted in passing, is the philosophical basis of the doctrine of immortality, whether Indian, Hebrew, or Greek.

The great identification, 'That art thou,' is stated in the form of another equation, namely, Brahman = Âtman, *e. g.*, 'This Âtman is Bráhman' (*Bṛh. Up.*, II, 5, 19). The pre-Upanishad de-

[1] Gen., I, 27. [2] Luke, III, 36. [3] *Belief in God*, p. 227.

[4] "The hope of a future life Jesus grounds upon man's essential kinship to God"—Stevens, *The Theology of the New Testament*, p. 99.

velopment of Bráhman has already been pointed out. It means, first, the word as embodied in hymn, formula, and text, whether the emphasis be objectively upon the word as something spoken or remembered, or subjectively upon the content and meaning of the word. But in the famous cosmological passage (Çat. Br., VI, 1, 1) Bráhman 'the threefold science' (*i. e.*, Rig-Veda, Sâma-Veda and Yajur-Veda) is regarded as the first born of Prajâpati, and as it were the creative programme. Hence Bráhman as the first born *Logos* 'poured itself forth and filled this whole world,' *i. e.*, the Logos objectified itself and became incarnate as the world of nature. So we have Bráhman the *World* standing over against Bráhman the *Word* as its manifestation, in Plato's language 'the sensible God' as 'the image of the intellectual.'[1] But in the Upanishads, Bráhman 'Word' is not only objectified and found in nature (*e. g.*, 'All this is Bráhman' Chând. Up., III, 14, 1), but is also as it were '*subjectified*' and found in the human heart. The doctrine of Bráhman in the heart appears in many passages, *e. g.*, 'This is my Âtman (self or ego) within the heart, this is Bráhman' (Chând. Up., III, 14, 4); 'Consciousness (prajñâ) is Bráhman' (Ait. Up., I, 3, 2); 'The heart is the highest Bráhman' (*Bṛh. Up.*, IV, 1, 7). Or again take the second member of the equation, namely, Âtman. Its derivation is disputed. Still the usage is elear enough. The word has the following meanings as correctly given by Deussen:[2] (1) one's own body in opposition to the outer world, (2) the trunk of the body in opposition to the limbs, (3) the soul in opposition to the body, and (4) the essential in opposition to the non-essential. All of these meanings may be illustrated from the Upanishads. The logical order would seem to be: (*a*) bodily self, (*b*) mental self, (*c*) universal self. Thus Âtman is the 'self' in the widest sense. The formula, 'Bráhman is Âtman,' would mean, then, that the objective reality (Bráhman) is the same as the subjective reality (Âtman). As we have it in the splendid passage (Chând. Up., III, 13, 7): 'That light which shines above this heaven, higher than all, higher than everything, in the highest world, beyond which there are no other worlds, that is *the same light* which is within man.' This identification is rendered possible, as al-

[1] *Timæus*, p. 515, Jowett's trans.

[2] *Geschichte*, S. 286.

ready pointed out, by converting Bráhman the *makrokosmos* into a *mikrokosmos*, and so conceiving it as consciousness or more properly as the knowing subject. This manipulation of the old cosmological Bráhman involves a peculiar psychological treatment at which we must briefly glance.

The psychology of the Upanishads is thoroughly idealistic. Thus in the dialogue between Ajâtaçatru King of Kâçi and Gârgya Bâlâki (*Bṛh. Up.*, II, 1, 17–20), we are told that when a person goes to sleep, then the knowing subject (*vijñânamaya puruṣa*) lies in the ether which is in the heart, having absorbed within itself all the knowledge of the senses. When asleep the person may dream, and so create for himself the worlds of dream-land, in which he may figure as a great king or a great Brâhman. Or his sleep may be dreamless, in which case all difference between subject and object is blotted out. *This is the very image of reality.* When he awakes, then from the knowing self emerge all senses, all worlds, all gods, all beings, *i. e.*, all the phenomena of actual or of possible existence, even as a spider from its thread, or as sparks from fire. Two doctrines are here clearly taught: (1) The essential ideality of all conscious experience, *i. e.*, 'the world is my idea,' and (2) no essential difference between the dream-state and the waking-state, *i. e.*, 'life is a dream.' In this way Bráhman, the objective world, is reduced to a mere world of ideas created by the human consciousness. On the principle that there is "no object without a subject," all beings, all gods, all worlds, all breaths, all souls, may be said to be contained in the self as spokes in the axle of a wheel (*Bṛh. Up.*, II, 5, 15). Thus all things become one in the self as consciousness (*prajñâtman* Kaush., III, 3–4).[1]

In a sense, then, all things become one in the conscious-self, but there still remains the dualism of subject and object. This must be resolved if possible. The quest for absolute reality was also the quest for absolute unity. For the Indian sages, such absolute unity and reality were symbolized by the states of dreamless sleep and death. Here there is no duality of subject and object. Knowledge

[1] With the Âtman as the ground of the unity of all knowledge Deussen compares Kant's doctrine of the synthetic unity of apperception.

there is, indeed; for "knowing is inseparable from the knower," because he is imperishable, and because it is the very nature of the knower to know; but "there is then no second, nothing else different from him that he could know," (*Bṛh. Up.*, IV, 3, 30). Some sort of transcendent consciousness seems to be implied in the paradoxical statement that "when (in that condition) he does not know, yet he is knowing, though he does not know." Here the soul is its own object, or, better, there is no distinction between subject and object, because the soul is like an ocean single and all-embracing. Like the one reality of Chând. Up., VI, 2, 1, the soul as the witnessing self is one without a second, because its sphere is Bráhman. This is one's true form, in which one is free from desire, free from evil, free from fear. This is the highest goal, the highest world, the highest bliss (*Bṛh. Up.*, IV, 3, 21–32). It may be noted in passing that consciousness (as we know it) was to the Indian thinker, as time and space to Schopenhauer, the principle of individuation. Being was one. Non-being took the form of multiplicity. And just as in Chând. Up., VI, 2, 1, 2, being was first postulated and then non-being attacked, so unity was postulated in the early prose Upanishads, while multiplicity was attacked in the later poetic sections, especially in *Bṛh. Up.*, IV, 4, 19 and *Kaṭh. Up.*, IV, 10, 11.

We come now to the nature and attributes of Bráhman. In Bṛh. Up., III, 9, 28[7] we read *vijñânam ânandam Brahma* "Bráhman is knowledge and bliss." And in the famous *Ânandavalli* of the Taitt. Up. the nature of Bráhman is described as *satyam jñânam ânandam*, "Reality, Thought, and Bliss." I read with Deussen ânandam 'bliss' instead of anantam 'infinite.' The reasons for the change are obvious. We have here clearly the germ of the later formula *sac-cid-ânanda*, "Being, Thought, and Bliss." Bráhman is further described as *ekam eva advitîyam*, "One only without a second." Thus far the characterization of Bráhman is positive. But in four passages of the *Bṛh. Up.* (III, 9, 26, IV, 2, 4, IV, 4, 22, IV, 5, 15) the absolute separation of Bráhman from everything which is changeable and knowable is emphasized. 'He is incomprehensible, for he cannot be comprehended, he is imperishable, for he cannot perish; he is unattached, for nothing attaches itself to him.' In a word, according to the doctrine of the great sage, *Yâjñavalkya*, the Self can only be described negatively as *neti neti*, "no, no." This may mean that the Self, like a mathematical infinite which is too great for any assignable quantity, is also too great for any assignable attribute, in which case '*neti neti*' would mean 'no, no,' in the sense of 'inadequate, inadequate.' That is, 'all determination is limitation.' Possibly Spinoza's distinction between definition by genus and definition by essence may help us here. If so, then Bráhman is defined through his essence, when he (or it) is described as Reality, Thought, and Bliss. However this may be, it is true that in many passages of the Upanishads the same attributes, both positive and negative, are applied to Bráhman as are applied to God in the Bible. Thus he is self-existent, unborn, eternal, ancient, unchanging, great, omnipresent, luminous, pure, bodiless, etc. (cf. *Kaṭh. Up.*, II, 18, 22, *Muṇḍ. Up.*, I, 1, 6, 7, II, 2, 1–11). But on the whole the emphasis rests on the 'natural' rather than on the 'moral' attributes, and these are put by preference in a negative rather than in a positive form.

The question arises, How can Bráhman be known? The attributes of Bráhman have been described. How were these determined? The Indian thinker, like Spinoza, began with the problem of the world as a whole. The cosmological Bráhman as the world of *extension* in its totality, was proved by the good old way of common-sense through external intuition. In other words, it was simply assumed. In like manner the psychological Bráhman as consciousness (Ait. Up., I, 3, 2,) or the world of *thought*, was proved by internal intuition. But beneath consciousness was something more fundamental still, the root of both the inner and the outer world, the unity of subject and object. It is at once the ground of knowing and of being. It is called 'the life of life, the eye of the eye, the ear of the ear, the mind of the mind' (*Bṛh. Up.*, IV, 4, 18). Whoso knows this knows Bráhman. But it is unknowable. For 'how,' asked *Yâjñavalkya* in the very spirit of Berkeley and Kant, 'should one know him through whom one knows all this? How, O beloved, should one know the *Knower?*' (*Bṛh. Up.*, II, 4, 13).

Here the way of intuition, whether external or internal, avails nothing. But we can detect the method of the discovery of these high doctrines. It is the dialectic of reason. It is the Socratic method of question and answer. Thus five theologians once came together and 'held a discussion as to what is our Self and what is Bráhman' (Chând. Up., V, 11, 1). The *Bṛhad-âraṇyaka Upanishad*, especially, is full of philosophical dialogues. The method is essentially the same as that by which Socrates elaborates the notion of the Good and Spinoza the notion of *Deus* or *Substantia*. After we have been taken behind the scenes, as it were, and have heard with our own ears thinkers like *Yâjñavalkya* and *Ajâtaçatru*, as they argue on these high themes, silence opponents, and establish the true doctrine of Bráhman, it is somewhat incongruous to find in the Upanishads (especially in the *Bṛh. Up.*) long lists of teachers through whom the doctrine of Bráhman is supposed to have been handed down in regular tradition. This is the point of view of the dogmatic Upanishads, in which there is a tendency to frown upon independent argumentation, and to make everything of the instruction of the capable teacher. 'That doctrine is not to be obtained by argument, but when it is declared by another, then it is easy to understand.' 'Unless it be taught by another, there is no way to it' (Kaṭh. Up., I, 2, 8–9). That is, the doctrine of Bráhman is something to be passively received and believed. It may be noted that only in the secondary and dogmatic stage of doctrine would the word 'upanishad' appropriately have the meaning of 'a sitting at the feet of a teacher,' and therefore passive acceptance of his teaching. The lists of teachers in the *Bṛh. Up.* go back even to Bráhman the self-existent. In a period when the work of the guru or teacher was so all-important, Bráhman himself was considered as the first of all gurus. So in the second or post-exile stage of O. T. religion the doctrine of God as teacher is emphasized. 'Teach me, O God' is a frequent thought in the Psalms of the period. Thus to sum up, there are virtually two forms of Bráhman. The first or lower form is knowable through sense perception and consciousness. We may compare it with the *natura naturata* of Spinoza viewed as an aggregate of finite modes. As conditioned it points to something beyond itself which is unconditioned.[1] The second or higher form of Bráhman is a postulate of reason. As identical with the knowing subject, it can never become an object of knowledge, and so must ever remain in its inmost nature a mystery. Being, unity, thought, and bliss may be predicated of it. But even here it may be that we must add the qualification *neti, neti*, 'inadequate, inadequate.' Still, however mysterious its nature may be, its existence can be known. Such an immanent reality, as the ground of all knowing and being, is suggested by consciousness; but, more than this, it is proved by the speculative insight of the ancient seers. And so, although Bráhman, the knowing subject, as such is unknowable, yet the doctrine of Bráhman may be handed down from teacher to teacher and received on faith by the believing pupil.

We have already discussed the doctrine of identity in the Upanishads. It is emphasized in a goodly number of passages. 'That light which shines above this heaven . . . is the same light which is within man' (Chând. Up., III, 13, 7). 'Brahman is Âtman.' 'That art thou.' Whatever is real in man or in nature is identical with Bráhman and there is no difference. Deep sleep and death are the image of reality. In them the finite consciousness as the principle of individuation has no sphere. In them the forms of cognition which make for multiplicity are transcended. Bráhman is described as 'thought.' Regard thought qualitatively instead of quantitatively, or in Kantian language eliminate the pure forms of intuition space and time, or blot out the finite consciousness while still regarding thought as persistent; and lo! thought is seen to be one and indivisible, the sole reality, and conscious of itself as bliss. It is from this high standpoint that Bráhman is described as reality, unity, thought, and bliss. All this according to the highest teaching of the Upanishads is eternally true. It is true for every man, yea for every creature. But alas! most creatures are like people who 'walk again and again over a gold treasure that has been hidden in the earth'[2]

[1] Cf. *Chând. Up.*, III, 13, 8.
[2] Cf. parable of the Hidden Treasure, Matt. XIII, 44.

(Chând. Up., VIII, 3, 2). They go day after day into the Bráhma-world (in deep sleep), and yet do not discover it. The soul's identity with Bráhman remains hidden from their eyes. This is the discovery of discoveries, the supreme discovery. Even the eternal Bráhman himself made this discovery in the beginning, saying *Aham Brahma asmi* 'I am Bráhman' (*Bṛh. Up.*, I, 4, 10). So Bráhman became what he is through knowledge. He knew himself as Bráhman and so became Bráhman. In like manner whosoever awakes to the same consciousness, whether deva or rishi or man, he too becomes Bráhman. The way of deliverance is the way of knowledge. 'He who knows Bráhman attains the highest' (Taitt. Up., II, 1). 'I am Bráhman!' 'I am a child of God!' So speaks the profoundest religious consciousness of both India and Palestine. And the consciousness which so speaks is conceived in both, albeit with far-reaching differences, as the result of a divine discovery, an awakening to reality, a realization of one's true self.

C. Consequences of the Doctrine.

The older Upanishads are integral parts of the *Âraṇyakas* or 'forest treatises.' These represent the speculations of men who, in secular phraseology, had 'retired from business,' or, in religious phraseology, had 'withdrawn from the world.' The doctrine of the four *âçramas* or stages of life, like that of the four castes, was of gradual growth. An early notice (Chând. Up., II, 23, 1) mentions only three generic duties of the Vedic Aryans: (*a*) that of sacrifice, study and almsgiving, (*b*) that of austerity (*tapas*), and (*c*) that of the *Brahmacârin* or student in the house of a teacher. These are brought forward as different types of religious life, which find their reward in the worlds of the blessed. Contrasted with these, however, is the state of the *Brahmasaṁstha*, 'he who stands fast in Bráhman,' who obtains immortality. This passage clearly dates from a time when the later distinction between four *âçramas* had not yet crystallized. In fact we have here perhaps the germ of such a fourfold division, for the three functions mentioned correspond to those of the *grihastha*, *vânaprastha* and *brahmacârin* respectively, while the *Brahmasaṁstha* as occupying the new or Upanishad standpoint, would seem to be an anticipation of the later *sannyâsin.*[1] Three of the four stages are entirely natural. Knowledge is acquired during the first twenty or thirty years of a man's life (Chând. Up., VI, 1, 2); after that come marriage and the duties of a householder; and finally as old age comes on men retire from active life, hand over their business to their children, and devote their last days to religious contemplation. For as Plato says,[2] "the time (*i. e.*, 50 years) has now arrived at which they must raise the eye of the soul to the universal light which lightens all things and behold the absolute good." To drop the cares of a householder would in India mean naturally to spend most of one's time in the cool and leafy forest on the outskirts of the village, or to wander in oriental simplicity from settlement to settlement of the same Aryan brotherhood, having one's few wants supplied by the hospitality of one's clan-people. This was no more begging than it is for the occidental to 'go visiting' where he knows that he will be asked to dine. In each community the 'superannuated,' especially priests and warriors, would often meet one another and talk over the themes which are naturally interesting to old men as they draw near to the end of life.[3] For them philosophy was in a very real sense 'a meditation of death.' Such discussions, however, were not confined to men. Women take part in them by asking questions (*e. g.*, Maitreyi, *Bṛh. Up.*, II, 4, and Gârgî, Ibid., III, 6 and 8). Nor were they confined to the circle of the aged. Just as Socrates in his search for truth delighted in catechizing young men (*e. g.*, Charmides), so the thinkers of ancient India were fond of asking young men how much they knew (Chând. Up., V, 3), especially if they had just returned from the house of the preceptor, well read and conceited (Chând. Up., VI, 1, 2, 3). Fathers teach their sons the doctrine of Bráhman (Chând. Up., VI). It is remarkable what a prominent part the Kshatriyas played in these discussions. Not only were there philosophical tournaments at

[1] Vid. Deussen in loco. (*Upanishads*, S. 96 ff.).
[2] *Republic*, Bk. VII, p. 244, Jowett's trans.
[3] Cf. *Chând. Up.*, I, 8, V, 11.

the courts of kings, *e. g.*, at the court of Janaka king of the Videhas (*Bṛh. Up.*, III, 1, 1), but the kings themselves were not infrequently philosophers, *e. g.*, Ajâtaçatru (*Bṛh. Up.*, VI, 1) and Açvapati Kaikeya (Chând. Up., V, 11, 4–5). Thus the ideal of Plato was realized that kings should be philosophers and philosophers kings. There were not only Brâhman sages, but Kshatriya sages also; and the latter are often represented as better acquainted with the doctrine of Bráhman than the former. *E. g.*, Pravâhana Jaivali (Chând. Up., I, 8, 2, V, 3, 5) and Açvapati Kaikeya (V, 11). It looks as if the philosophic movement represented by the earliest Upanishads had derived its impulse originally from the Kshatriya thinkers. In this connection it is interesting to remember that both Buddha and Krishna are represented as royal sages. From all this it is clear that the doctrine of Bráhman was no secret doctrine of a philosophic coterie, as the current explanation of Upanishad would suggest, but was communicated to anyone, Brâhman or Kshatriya, old or young, man or woman, who was worthy to receive it. But as regards its origin, it must be referred decidedly to the class of vânaprasthas or men who had either partially or wholly retired from active life and so had leisure for thought. There is no instance, so far as I know, of two young men or two women discussing the doctrine of Bráhman. Whenever a young man or a woman takes part in a dialogue, the other speaker is invariably either a Brâhman sage or a Kshatriya sage. 'Advanced thought,' then, in Ancient India came from the circle of the vânaprasthas or 'forest-dwellers.' In many respects it was radical and revolutionary. It involved reconstruction and readjustment in several directions. It had important consequences, religious, ethical, eschatological, and philosophical. There must now be considered.

I. Religious.

The religion of the Upanishads is the religion of the Âtman or Self. 'The Self is the lord of all beings, the king of all beings,' (*Bṛh. Up.*, II, 5, 15). '*Let a man worship the Self alone as dear*' (I, 4, 8). This is perhaps the nearest approach in the early Upanishads to the doctrine of love to God as set forth in the command, "Thou shall love the Lord thy God." The Self is nearer and dearer than son or wealth or anything else, because it is the Self and is manifested to the consciousness of every one as his own soul. As *Yâjñavalkya* beautifully says: 'A wife is not dear, that you may love the wife; *but that you may love the Self*, therefore a wife is dear' (*Bṛh. Up.*, II, 4, 5). This is not to be regarded as the statement of an extreme egoism, but rather as something involved in the great doctrine of identity. If the religion of the Vedas is to be described as objective and ritualistic, that of the Upanishads must be described as subjective and spiritual. It is a religion not of the object but of the subject. God is sought not beyond the stars, but in the depths of the human heart. The identity of the individual self and of the Highest Self is recognized. Being able to say 'I am Bráhman,' one becomes Bráhman.

> He who the Self within himself
> Beholds as God immediately,
> Lord of the future and the past,—
> He from that time is not afraid.
>
> (*Bṛh. Up.*, IV, 4, 15).

The worship of the Self looks at first sight like self-worship. But it would hardly be fair to call it that. The Christian doctrine of the Spirit of God, the Holy Spirit, as dwelling in the heart of the devout believer and so creating a mystic union between the human and the Divine, is perhaps the best analogue of the doctrine in question. This is the standpoint of Paul the Apostle. Religion began with him when Christ was revealed *in* him.[1]

In the early Upanishads we notice a polemic against the worship of the Devas. The objections are metaphysical. Each object or phenomenon is an effect of the Self and so only partially and inadequately expresses the nature thereof. 'The Self is unseen. . . . As breathing he is called breath, as speaking speech, as seeing eye, as hearing ear, as thinking thought. All these are but names of his works. Whoso worships one or other of these

[1] *Gal.*, I, 16.

is not wise; for the Self is only partially identical with any one of them. Let one worship the Self alone; for in him all these become one' (*Bṛh. Up.*, I, 4, 7). But the antithesis between the Self and his works is also the antithesis between subject and object. 'He who worships another deity, thinking that the deity is one and he another, is not wise.' To be able to say, 'I am Bráhman,' is to become the self of all things, yea even of the Devas (*Bṛh. Up.*, I, 4, 10). The same sharp polemic against the popular worship is expressed in Kena I, 5:

> Unthinkable by thought is that
> Through which they say that thought is thought;
> Bráhman know that alone to be,
> Not that which people here adore.

It is worthy of notice that both the sages of India and the prophets of Israel attacked the popular worship of their times. The former assailed it on metaphysical grounds; the latter (*e. g.*, Amos and Hosea) on moral grounds.

There was finally a compromise between the religion of the Âtman and the religion of the Devas. The religion of the Devas flourished among the people at large, while the religion of the Âtman prevailed among the Vânaprasthas and such as came under their influence. The Atman was a 'jealous god,' and tolerated no second. For the thinkers of India an 'associate' of the Âtman was as obnoxious metaphysically as an associate of Allâh was for Mohammed religiously. The Âtman swallowed up the Vedic Devas and so became 'all in all.' It then retired beyond the reach of mortal ken. The one reality was made unknowable. As we have it paradoxically in Kena II, 3:

> By whom not thought, by him 'tis thought;
> By whom 'tis thought, he knows it not.
> Unknowable for those that know,
> Well known by those who do not know!

This sounds somewhat like the N. T. paradox of the things hidden from the wise and prudent and revealed unto babes. Here the early Upanishad doctrine of the unknowableness of the knowing subject is pushed to such an extreme as seriously to encroach upon the doctrine of deliverance through the knowledge of Bráhman. The result is that the unknowable Bráhman comes to be represented more and more by symbols. The syllable *Om*, the everlasting 'yea and amen' (Chând. Up., I, 1, 8), is a favorite emblem of Bráhman. So are *jyotis* 'light' (*Bṛh. Up.*, IV, 4, 16), and *prâṇa* 'breath,' 'spirit' (Chând. Up., IV, 10, 5).[1] But even more concrete symbols are employed.[2] And in the late dogmatic and sectarian Upanishads a whole host of deities, *e. g.*, *Brahmâ*, *Vishnu*, *Çiva*, *Nârâyaṇa*, etc., appear as representatives or personifications of Bráhman. Thus the Vedic deities are first banished and then either they or their equivalents are recalled to act as intermediaries between 'the Great Unknown' (Bráhman) and the conscious self. So there was a compromise between philosophy and popular religion in the period of the later Upanishads, just as there was between prophecy and popular religion among the Hebrews of the post-exile period.

II. Ethical.

The ethical system of the Upanishads is involved in the doctrine of Bráhman. And since we have in the Upanishads the identity of philosophy and religion, we may call the ethics found there both philosophical and religious. As philosophical, it is a deduction from the nature of Bráhman; as religious, a program for the attainment of Bráhman. Bráhman or the Self is the home of reality, thought, and bliss. It is far removed from multiplicity and change. It is beyond hunger, thirst, sorrow, delusion, old age, and death (*Bṛh. Up.*, III, 5, 1). It is sinless (Chând. Up., VIII, 7, 1). It is immortal. Whatever is separate from it is *sorrowful* (*Bṛh. Up.*, III, 7, 23). We stand here at the very birthplace of Indian pessimism. It is often referred to the influence of climatic and other natural conditions. Why then did pessimism not appear earlier in India? There is no clear trace of it either in the *Vedas* or in the *Brâhmaṇas*. It seems to me

[1] Compare 'God is light' (I John I, 5) and 'God is spririt' John IV, 24.

[2] *E. g.*, Indra in *Ait. Up.*, 1, 3, 14 [Deussen's numbering], *Kaush.*, III, 1, *Taitt.* I, 4.

that Oldenberg[1] is entirely in harmony with the sources when he assigns to Indian pessimism a speculative and metaphysical origin. There is a dam (Chând. Up., VIII, 4, 1) separating between the noumenal world which is timeless, changeless, sinless, and deathless, and the phenomenal world which is the home of unreality, multiplicity, decay, sin, sorrow, and death. To be on this side is *ipso facto* to be in the state of sorrow, for everything other than Bráhman is sorrowful. It is not that this world is the worst possible world, but that the world of Bráhman is so much better. As Oldenberg says,[2] "The glorification of the Âtman becomes involuntarily an ever increasingly bitter criticism of this world." Weighed against the changeless bliss of the Atman, the best that this changing world can afford must appear defective. A kind of pessimism has ever marked the attitude of the choicest spirits toward the actual world. We detect it in the writings of the Hebrew prophets, and also in the words of Jesus Christ and His Apostles, not to mention Plato and the moderns, Schopenhauer and Carlyle. The pessimism of the Indian sages is speculative and is the consequence of their theory of being; that of the Hebrew prophets is ethical, the consequence of their theory of duty.

The logical result of the condemnation of the world was its *renunciation*. The motive of such renunciation was declared to be the knowledge of the Self. Knowing this Self, Brâhmans give up the desire of children, wealth, and the world, and wander about as beggars (*Bṛh. Up.*, III, 5, 1). But renunciation in order to be genuine involves the destruction of desire, or rather the destruction of desires through the realization of one supreme desire. So we read of him who is without desire, free from desire, whose desire is realized, whose desire is the Self (*Bṛh. Up.*, IV, 4, 6). Such an one bears the name *akâmayamâna*, 'he who does not desire.'

> When all desires have been removed,
> Which make their home in human hearts,
> Mortal immortal then becomes,
> Bráhman e'en here is then attained.
>
> (*Bṛh. Up.*, IV, 4, 7.)

[1] *Buddha*, p. 42, ff. [2] *Op. cit.*, p. 42.

Likewise said Christ: "If any man would come after me, let him *deny* himself. . . . What doth it profit a man if he gain the whole world and lose his own soul." [1]

Not only is 'the world with its affections and lusts' to be renounced, but *union* with Bráhman the Self is to be realized. The name for such union is *sâyujya* and perhaps also *yoga*. The word '*yoga*' occurs only once in the older Upanishads (Taitt., II, 4, 1), and there in the sense of 'devotion.' But it came in course of time to be about equivalent to 'means of union.' Two such means have already been considered, namely knowledge and renunciation. In the later Upanishads, however, *yoga*, as actually used, refers to a very special kind of means connected with the control of the breath. As a way of realizing union (*sâyujya*) with deity, such control is first mentioned in *Bṛh. Up.*, I, 5, 23. From the control of the breath and senses resulted oftentimes the induction of a state of trance or unconsciousness. As we have it in the earliest account of the developed Yoga:

> For outer sense exists no form of Bráhman,
> Not with the eye can anyone behold him;
> But only through the spirit's high equipment,
> Whoso thus knows him, he becomes immortal.
>
> When the five senses quiet are,
> And with them also human thought;
> When functions intellect no more,
> This is known as the highest state.
>
> (*Kaṭh. Up.*, VI, 9, 10.)

The origin of this method of union is not difficult to detect. Bráhman, as the synthesis of subject and object, was best symbolized by the state of unconsciousness as seen in deep sleep and death. And besides Bráhman had come more and more to be regarded as theoretically unknowable. The finite consciousness, too, was regarded as at once the principle of *individuation* and of *desire*. In order to transcend these one must transcend consciousness. Only thus would renunciation be complete. What, then, more natural than to seek to be conformed to the

[1] Matt. XVI, 24–26.

image of Bráhman by the way of mysticism and trance through an artificial induction of the unconscious or perhaps of the *superconscious* state? All this reminds one of Neo-platonism. Ethics, then, in the Upanishads belongs to the soteriology of the religion of the Âtman. In this soteriology three moments have been distinguished, namely *knowledge* through speculative insight, *renunciation* and *mysticism*.

III. Eschatological.

The doctrine of transmigration first appears explicitly in the Upanishads. It is unknown in the Rig-Veda, where we meet only with the belief in a continued existence after death in the abode of Yama. It is true that the word *punarmṛtyu* 'Wiedertod,' 'second death,' occurs in the *Brâhmaṇas* as well as in *Bṛh. Up.*, I, 2, 7, etc.,[1] but there is clearly no reference to transmigration. The origin of Indian metempsychosis is uncertain. Gough[2] thinks that it was borrowed from the aborigines, because it has been shown to be a wide-spread belief among semi-savage tribes, and, moreover, was unknown in the pre-Upanishad literature. But another hypothesis is possible. May there not have been something in the Upanishad speculations of such a character as to give rise to the doctrine? The doctrine was clearly lifted into prominence by the *vânaprasthas*, who would hardly have picked up and cherished a non-Aryan superstition unless their own system of thought came to demand it. It seems to me that the advanced thought of the Upanishads called naturally for some revision of old eschatological conceptions. 'What is it that does not leave a man after death?' asked the son of *Ritabhâga* of *Yâjñavalkya*. 'Name' and 'work' he replied, *i. e.*, the knowing subject and his character. For 'a man becomes good by good work and bad by bad work' (*Bṛh. Up.*, III, 2, 12, 13). This position is still further developed in IV, 4, 2–6, where we read that after all multiplicity of sensation has ceased at the death of a man, then his *knowledge* (*vidyâ* consciousness of duty) and his *work* (*karman*), yea his whole previous experience (*pûrvaprajñâ*), lay

[1] 'He overcomes the second death,' cf. Apocal. Ioh. II, 11.

[2] *Philosophy of the Upanishads*, pp. 24, 25.

hold of him and lead him to another form of existence, whether it be that of the fathers, or of the Gandharvas or of the Devas or of Prajâpati or of Bráhman *or of other beings.* Thus the motive which governs these speculations is ethical. The law which everywhere operates is the law of recompense. 'Whatsoever a man soweth that shall he also reap.' The future world of the old Vedic teaching is no longer conceived as 'the place of departed spirits' without regard to character, but is broken up into 'spheres of recompense,' in which there are different degrees of dignity and blessedness corresponding to 'the deeds done in the body.' The future state was not regarded as a disembodied state. Each one there had his own *rûpa* or 'form,' perhaps conceived as a 'spiritual body.'[1] But the world of Yama had come to be regarded as exclusively the world of the blessed. What was to be done with those who were not worthy of entering that world? 'Hell' had not yet been invented as a place of punishment. Let it be remembered that the spheres of recompense began at the top with the very world of Bráhman himself (*Brahmaloka*). What more natural than to extend them downward until they include the worlds of men, animals, plants, and inorganic nature? According to this view, the doctrine of transmigration in India began through the extension of the 'spheres of recompense,' so as to cover all beings, all forms, all bodies. This seems to me a very plausible hypothesis. Accordingly there would be a future form and condition appropriate for every creature. The sage might take the form of a Deva, while the man whose conduct had been evil would be born as 'a dog or a hog or a *Chaṇḍâla*' (Chând. Up., V, 10, 7). Here, as in Plato, transmigration is conceived as a minister of justice, which assigns to every creature its appropriate lot. The law of man's nature and destiny is expressed as follows: 'Man is altogether made of desire;[2] as is his desire, so is his insight;[3] as is his insight so is his work (*karman*); and as is his work so is his destiny' (*Bṛh. Up.*, IV, 4, 5). All this is true for human experience and

[1] Cf. *prâṇaçarîra* 'whose body is spirit,' *Chând. Up.*, III, 14, 2.

[2] *Kâma*, cf. the '*conatus*' of Spinoza and the 'will to live' of Schopenhauer.

[3] *Kratu* = both intellect and will.

thought, but for them alone. In Kantian language the law of *karman* is a principle regulative of experience, but not constitutive of reality. For as soon as the standpoint of human consciousness which is marked by desire and ignorance is transcended, then both merit and demerit vanish into thin air. This, it seems to me, was the earliest form of the post-Vedic eschatology. It furnished a favorite field for speculation, so that very soon numerous modifications were introduced into the older doctrine. As pointed out by Deussen,[1] these modifications proceed by way of the combination and recombination of the fundamental eschatological conceptions under the domination of different motives, ethical, ritualistic and cosmological. As might be expected, their details cannot always be harmonized.

It is a well-known fact that in the later Vedântism philosophy is often conceived negatively as a means of deliverance from the round of transmigration. It cannot be too much emphasized that in the beginning it was not so. For the thinkers of the earliest Upanishads, the investigation of Bráhman, the one reality, was something positive. Their impulse to philosophy was not derived from belief in transmigration, but rather the doctrine of transmigration itself seems to have been, if not the product of the doctrine of Bráhman, at least an ethical postulate of the same course of thought which led to the developed doctrine of Bráhman. For it expressed the conviction of an indissoluble wedlock between character and destiny.

IV. Philosophical.

The doctrine of *Mâyâ* is the logical result of the doctrine of Bráhman. Bráhman, like the *substantia* of Spinoza, is one and indivisible; so the speculative reason of India declared. But for sense multiplicity exists and is real. There is thus a dualism between reason and sense. The one affirms unity; the other multiplicity. It has been evident from the very first that multiplicity must go to the wall. The temper of the Vedânta thinkers has ever been rationalistic.

[1] *Upanishads*, S. 139 ff.

For a long time the antithesis between unity and plurality remained unresolved. The two stood side by side unarticulated and unreconciled. From the very first, however, the explanation was implicit. It may be stated almost in the terms of the Eleatic school. Being is : non-being is not. Being is one : non-being is many. Therefore multiplicity is not. It is unreal. It is an accident pertaining to human consciousness, not something constitutive of reality. In a word, it is *Mâyâ* 'illusion.' Such was the final explanation.

The word '*mâyâ*,' from *mâ* to measure, effect, make, occurs many times in the Rig-Veda in the sense of *power*, especially wonderful, supernatural or creative power. In the plural it means 'supernatural arts' or 'devices,' as in RV., VI, 47, 18, VIII, 14, 14, etc. *Mâyâ* does not occur in the oldest Upanishads except in *Bṛh. Up.*, II, 5, 19 (= RV., VI, 47, 18). Thus :

> He found his form in every form incarnate,
> This is the form of him for human vision ;
> Through *magic* wanders multiform wise Indra,
> Yoked are his horses by the tens and hundreds.

This passage seems to furnish the starting point for the later use of *mâyâ*. Indra becomes *multiform* through his *supernatural arts*. Multiplicity is made the effect of mâyâ, and mâyâ may here be rendered by 'magic' just as well as by 'power.' In the Çvet. Up., occurs the first passage in which mâyâ is used in a cosmic sense :

> From whom come hymns, works, vows, and sacrifices,
> Future and past, yea all the Veda-teachings,
> He as *Magician* (mâyin) all this world created,
> In which the soul through *mâyâ* is entangled.

> *Mâyâ* know *prakriti* (= nature) to be,
> And as *Enchanter* the Great God ;
> With that which of his parts consists,
> Pervaded is the entire world. (IV, 9, 10.)

In this sense the word '*mâyâ*' is often used in the sectarian Upanishads and in the Bhagavadgîtâ.

We have, then, in the Upanishads three moments in the development of the relation between the one and the many: (1) the thesis, unity is (Chând. Up., VI, 2, 1), (2) the antithesis, plurality is not (*Kaṭh. Up.*, IV, 10, 11), and (3) the synthesis, plurality is the illusive play of unity, the magic of Bráhman the great magician (Çvet. Up., IV, 9, 10). As the source of all sound doctrine Bráhman appeared in the early Upanishads as the *Great Teacher;* while as the source of all (apparent) multiplicity he appears in the late Upanishads as the *Great Magician.*

Concerning the antiquity of the doctrine of mâyâ, Colebrooke[1] says: "I take it to be no tenet of the original Vedântin philosophy;" while on the contrary Gough[2] claims "that mâyâ is part and parcel of the primitive Indian cosmological conception, as exhibited in the Upanishads themselves." Which is right? It seems to me that each is both right and wrong. Colebrooke is right in the sense that the doctrine of mâyâ is not found explicitly stated in the older Upanishads; while Gough is right in the sense that the doctrine in question is involved in the doctrine of Bráhman, the great theme of all the Upanishads.[3]

[1] *Essays*, p. 242.

[2] *Upanishads*, p. xi.

[3] There is an interesting N. T. parallel. The net result of the New Testament theologically is the conception of God the Father, Christ, and the Holy Spirit. But these were left by the N. T. writers standing over against one another, philosophically unrelated and unexplained. The Greek theologians took up the problem and answered it by the doctrine of the *Trinity*. This doctrine is and is not a doctrine of the New Testament in the same sense in which mâyâ both is and is not a doctrine of the Upanishads. Neither is found explicitly in the documents in question, but on the other hand each seems to be implied.

CHAPTER IV.

THE DOCTRINE OF BRÁHMAN IN THE VEDÂNTA-SÛTRAS AS EXPOUNDED BY ÇANKARÂCÂRYA.

The period of the classical Upanishads was the creative period of Indian philosophy. It was naturally followed by an age of exposition and system-building. The earliest systematic statement of the doctrine of the Upanishads is found in the Vedânta-Sûtras. But these without a commentary are unintelligible. This want is supplied by the famous *Bhâṣya* of Çankarâcârya, the earliest extant commentary on the Vedânta-Sûtras. Here then we must take up the thread of our investigation. We shall cite from the excellent translation of Professor Thibaut.

Indian philosophy began with the problem of the universe as a whole. Purusha (RV., X, 90, 2), Prajâpati (Çat. Br., V, 1, 1, 4), and Brahman (Chând. Up., III, 14, 1), representing respectively the Vedic, the Brahmanic and the Upanishad speculation, are each of them identified with the totality of nature (*idam sarvam*). But this was little more than to fix the problem. It remained to reduce the chaos of existence to an ordered system through the insight of reason. As already pointed put, the Upanishads recognize different degrees of reality. There is, however, a tendency to employ the principle of dichotomy, to bring things under the head of either of two mutually exclusive categories. Not to mention the Vedic *sat* 'being' and *asat* 'non-being' which only gradually came to be used in sharp antithesis to each other, we have in the early Upanishads Brahman as the totality of things divided into Brahman with a form and Brahman formless, Brahman mortal and Brahman immortal, Brahman phenomenal and Brahman noumenal (*Bṛh. Up.*, II, 3, 1), Brahman defined and Brahman undefined, Brahman conditioned and Brahman unconditioned (Taitt. Up., II, 6), Brahman as time and Brahman as the timeless (Mait. Up., VI, 15). In like manner Spinoza began with the conception of nature in its totality and concreteness

(*Tractatus Brevis*, I, 2), but soon distinguished between *Natura Naturans* (= Deus, Substantia, Natura *par excellence*) and *natura naturata*, the world of finite modes. We may also cite the Kantian distinction between noumenon and phenomenon, and that of Schopenhauer between will and idea. We have already indicated how in the Upanishads the development of the relation between the one and the many passed through three stages: (1) Unity is, (2) Plurality is not, and (3) Plurality is the illusive play of unity. In the place of the early distinction between Brahman noumenal and Brahman phenomenal, we have finally the distinction between Brahman and mâyâ, in which mâyâ takes the place of the phenomenal Brahman and is regarded as non-being as opposed to Being or Brahman. This is the standpoint of Çankarâcârya.

A. *The Theology of Çankarâcârya.*

In the introduction to his great work on the Vedânta-Sûtras, Çankara makes a sharp distinction between subject and object, ego and non-ego. The one is the home of intelligence and reality; the other, of the non-intelligent and the unreal. Ordinary experience (*vyavahâra*) is the result of superimposing the non-ego upon the Ego, the unreal upon the Real. Thus, as Çankara says, 'on the Self are superimposed particular conditions such as caste, stage of life, age, outward circumstances, and so on.' These particular conditions are called *upâdhis* or 'limiting adjuncts.' On them are based all the practical distinctions of life. They are the ground of multiplicity. By them the unity of the Self is fictitiously broken up. Remove them, and lo the residue is pure thought untainted by the antithesis of subject and object, or by the distinction of 'this' and 'that.' Superimposition (*adhyâsa*) is said to be 'a natural procedure' on the part of man, since it is involved in all functioning of the intellect. It is the subjective principle of multiplicity. As such it inheres in the human mind as a transcendental form of cognition just as time and space, according to Kant and Schopenhauer.

But superimposition is called not only 'a natural procedure,' but also one 'which has its source in *wrong knowledge*' (*mithyâ-*

jñâna) namely, failure to discriminate between subject and object. We have here a kind of metaphysical or rather transcendental 'depravity,' which is at once 'racial' affecting all men and 'total' affecting the entire thought of every man. This 'total depravity' of the *intellect* is the Indian analogue of the 'total depravity' of the *will* as held by a certain school of Christian thinkers. Nescience or non-knowledge (*avidyâ*) is the name given to this transcendental depravity of the intellect, since it persists in superimposing the unreal *apâdhis* or 'limiting adjuncts' upon the one reality, and so creating the appearance of multiplicity. Knowledge (*vidyâ*), on the other hand, is the discrimination of the Self from the not-self, the Real from the unreal. The world of ordinary experience (*lokavyavahâra*) is regarded as the sphere of Nescience. According to the Indian thinker, to know individuals, houses, trees, and such things is to know nothing as one ought to know. Çankara does not say that for one who knows nothing higher such knowledge may not have the value of reality. Indeed, he tells us plainly that 'the entire complex of phenomenal existence is considered as true as long as the knowledge of Brahman being the Self of all has not arisen; just as the phantoms of a dream are considered to be true until the sleeper wakes' (II, 1, 14). And from this point of view he refutes the idealism and nihilism of the Buddhists in language which makes him almost seem to be a realist (II, 2, 28–32). Thus, according to Çankara, there are two kinds of reality, the first practical, phenomenal, relative (*vyâvahârika*), and the second noumenal and absolute (*pâramârthika*). And corresponding to these, there are two kinds of knowledge: 'wrong knowledge' (*mithyâjñâna*) the correlative of phenomenal reality, and 'perfect knowledge' (*samyagjñâna*) the correlative of absolute reality. To identify oneself with the first or lower reality is to become 'a part of nature,' subject to the law of *samsâra*, the eternal sequence of moral causation. But, on the other hand, to identify oneself with the second or higher reality is to transcend the sphere of merit and demerit and to realize the unity and blessedness of Brahman the Highest.

The theory of the superimposition of 'limiting adjuncts' leads naturally to the doctrine of the identity of the individual self and the Highest Self. For Çankara, as for Kant, space (*âkâça*) is one. But it may be broken up into spaces by earthen jars and the like. As Space is to spaces, so is the Supreme Self to individual selfs. As Çankara puts it: 'Just as the spaces within jars, if considered apart from their limiting conditions, are merged in universal space, so the soul, which exists in all bodies, if considered apart from the limiting adjuncts, is nothing else but the highest Self' (I, 3, 7). Thus 'the Lord differs from the soul, which is embodied, acts and enjoys, and is the product of Nescience, in the same way as the real juggler, who stands on the ground differs from the illusive juggler, who, holding in his hand a shield and a sword, climbs up to the sky by means of a rope; or as the free unlimited ether differs from the ether of a jar' (I, 1, 17). In short, the difference between the individual self and the highest Self, while valid for the lower point of view, is not valid for the higher. From the standpoint of the highest reality it is 'fictitious.' Before leaving this point we may glance at the analogous New Testament doctrine. God is declared to be spirit (πνεῦμα, John IV, 24). But πνεῦμα in the N. T. sometimes indicates the human spirit and sometimes the Divine Spirit.[1] Possessing or rather being 'spirit' is the link between the human and the Divine. The reference of πνεῦμα to the Divine is made explicit by such expressions as 'the Spirit of God,' 'the Spirit of Christ,' 'the *Holy* Spirit'; just as, when *âtman* refers to the one Spirit or Self, it is often enlarged to *Paramâtman*, 'the *Highest* Self.' We even have in the Pauline writings a kind of doctrine of identity, namely, the personal confession of Paul the mystic in Gal. II, 20: 'It is no longer I that live, but Christ liveth in me.'

Perhaps the most characteristic as well as speculatively the highest doctrine of Çankarâcârya is the doctrine of the '*double nature* of Bráhman, according as it is the object either of knowledge or of Nescience' (I, 1, 11). We have already referred to passages in the Upanishads (*Bṛh.*, II, 3, 1, *Taitt.*, II, 6), which would seem to furnish the starting point for such a distinction. The doctrine in question is the outcome of a consistent and

[1] So with *rûah* 'spirit' in the O. T.

thoroughgoing application of the theory of limiting adjuncts. As already explained, if we think away the *upâdhis*, there remains only pure being which is pure thought, one and absolute. This is at once the standpoint and the method of deliverance (*moksha*). For 'as soon as, in consequence of the declaration of non-difference contained in such passages as "that art thou," the conviction of non-difference comes to consciousness, the transmigratory state of the individual soul and the creative quality of Brahman vanish at once, the whole phenomenon of plurality, which springs from wrong knowledge, being sublated by perfect knowledge' (II, 1, 22). We have here at once a doctrine of scripture and a doctrine of faith. Just as the Christian is to 'reckon himself (*ethically*) dead unto sin, but alive unto God' on the basis of the scripture to this effect (Rom. VI, 11), even so the Vedântist is to reckon himself *metaphysically* separate from all plurality and identical with Brahman the 'one only without a second' on the basis of such scripture texts as *Tat tvam asi* 'that art thou.' So much for the man of 'perfect knowledge' who has attained to the perfect vision (*samyagdarçana*) or intuition (*pratyakṣa*) of the Highest Self. But what of the unenlightened multitudes who know not Brahman and yet profess to know and worship him as God? To answer this, we must remember that the law of the *upâdhis* governs all functioning of the intellect, ideation as well as sense-perception. To think at all is to think in terms of the 'limiting adjuncts,' or, as Kant would say, under the forms of space and time. Ideas, then, as well as percepts obey the law of the *upâdhis*, and the highest Idea, *i. e.*, God, just as much as any lower idea. But as already pointed out, the superimposition of the upâdhis, although a necessity of mind, is regarded as having its source in wrong knowledge. This transcendental 'depravity' of intellect taints all thought and all the objects of thought, even the highest object God, with the taint of unreality. The thinkable is unreal: the unthinkable alone is real.

> Unthinkable by thought is that
> Through which they say that thought is thought;
> Brahman know that alone to be,
> Not that which people here adore. (Kena, I, 5.)

By whom not thought by him 'tis thought;
By whom 'tis thought, he knows it not. (Kena, II, 3.)

Brahman is accordingly apprehended under two forms, first as qualified, defined, clothed upon with attributes, through the inevitable tendency of the mind to superimpose 'limiting conditions' on all the objects of its thought. As such it constitutes the anthropomorphic deity of popular worship, and so as an 'object of devotion' is localized in heaven, in the heart and so on. But, secondly, Brahman may be apprehended as separate from all limiting adjuncts whatever, as pure, unqualified, unattached, absolute. Of that ultimate mystery one can only say *neti neti* 'no, no.' Attributes such as infinite, eternal, unchangeable, omnipotent, omniscient, etc., are inapplicable, since they all presuppose connection with a spatial or temporal order. Even the characterization of Brahman as unity, reality, thought and bliss, is impossible, if this point of view be held rigorously, since these are all concepts derived from experience. In a word, as the final product of abstraction carried to the uttermost limits we have the concept of an absolute entity concerning which not a single predication can legitimately be made. The world of experience, which is usually regarded as the sphere of *science*, is here made the sphere of *nescience*, while that transcendent being concerning which we can say absolutely nothing, is called 'an object of knowledge'! What then is the relation between the 'higher' and the 'lower' Brahman? Both are the same and yet not the same. The higher Brahman = the lower Brahman minus the limiting adjuncts, while the lower Brahman = the higher Brahman plus the limiting adjuncts. Ultimate reality conceived anthropomorphically is the lower Brahman. Ultimate reality deanthropomorphized is the higher Brahman. The one, like the *Vorstellung* of Hegel, is a representation projected by the religious imagination; the other, like the *Begriff* of the same thinker, is a concept of reason. The lower knowledge (*aparâ vidyâ*) is concerned with the lower Brahman as the supreme concept of religion; while the higher knowledge (*parâ vidyâ*) is concerned with the higher Brahman as the supreme concept of philosophy.

We come finally to the cosmology of Çankarâcârya. As already explained, that form of Brahman which, according to the Upanishads, is mortal, phenomenal, defined, conditioned and subject to time and space, namely, Brahman as the ordered world of experience (*natura naturata*), is in Çankara's system virtually called Mâyâ. What is the relation of Mâyâ to Brahman? Çankara says in one place: 'Although all qualities are denied to Brahman, we nevertheless may consider it to be endowed with powers, if we assume in its nature an element of plurality, which is the mere figment of Nescience' (II, 1, 31); and in another place: 'By that element of plurality which is the fiction of nescience, which is characterized by name and form, which is evolved as well as non-evolved, which is not to be defined either as the existing or the non-existing, Brahman becomes the basis of this entire apparent world with its changes and so on, while in its true and real nature it at the same time remains unchanged, lifted above the phenomenal universe' (II, 1, 27); and once more: 'Belonging to the self, as it were, of the omniscient Lord, there are name and form, the figments of Nescience, not to be defined either as being nor as different from it, the germs of the entire expanse of the phenomenal world, called in Çruti and Smriti the illusion (*mâyâ*), power (*çakti*), or nature (*prakriti*) of the omniscient Lord' (II, 1, 14). These passages give the cosmological theory of Çankara, which we may briefly summarize as follows:

1. The universe consists of something which is neither the same as Brahman nor different. Objectively considered, it is *prakriti* 'matter' and *çakti* 'force.' But matter and force, while true for experience, cannot be true in the sphere of absolute reality (*paramârthatas*). Therefore, subjectively considered, the universe is *avidyâ* 'nescience' and *mâyâ* 'illusion.' It is 'the world as idea,' which has no existence except for consciousness. As consisting of the aggregate of the *upâdhis*, the world of experience belongs to the nature of the lower Brahman, *i. e.*, Brahman as 'fictitiously connected with mâyâ' (II, 2, 2).

2. Between the world of the upâdhis or 'finite modes' and the lower Brahman there intervene 'name and form' (*nâmarûpe*),

which are conceived both as ideally present even before the creation (I, 1, 5) in the knowledge of (the lower) Brahman as Creator, and as the highest categories of human experience. With the Indian conception of 'name and form' we may compare Spinoza's two attributes of Thought and Extension, which are regarded as bridging the gulf between the one infinite Substance and the multiplicity of finite modes. Çankara is also acquainted with the distinction between individual (*vyakti*) and species (*âkṛti* = εἶδος). The former he regards as coming into existence, but the latter as eternal (I, 3, 28). The *âkṛtayas* of Çankara are analogous to the Ideas of Plato and possibly to the Essences of Spinoza. Hence on the basis of relation to the world of experience we might arrange a series in a descending scale after the manner of the Gnostic emanations. Thus: (*a*) the higher Brahman separate from mâyâ, (*b*) the lower Brahman connected with mâyâ, (*c*) name and form, the revelation of mâyâ, (*d*) eternal species, (*e*) finite individuals.

3. Mâyâ is neither being nor non-being, but rather a *becoming*. It is not identical with the pure Brahman as the *Ding an sich*; nor is it, on the other hand, absolutely unreal, since it is real to consciousness. We have here to do with the Vedântic doctrine of development. Çankara speaks of a 'causal potentiality' (*bîjçakti* I, 4, 3) as the antecedent condition of the present ordered world. 'Without it the highest Lord could not be conceived as creator, as he could not become active if he were destitute of the potentiality of action.' Such 'causal potentiality' has 'the highest Lord for its substratum' and is 'of the nature of an illusion' (*mâyâmayî*). Here then we have the doctrine of a world-process grounded in Brahman as the highest Lord, real for sense, but unreal for reason, and so in its deepest nature illusory. It is to be noted that Brahman when related to the world is *ipso facto* the lower Brahman, as opposed to the higher or unrelated Brahman; thus, as the first term in the world-process (noumenal A), the lower Brahman quite properly bears the name of *Parameçvara*, 'the highest Lord.' The lower Brahman is just as real and just as unreal as the phenomenal world, since it is part and parcel of it. It is the ultimate *causal* abstraction to which thought naturally and inevitably tends. Like Kant's

Ideal of pure reason, the concept of the highest Lord as the great first cause has validity only as a principle 'regulative' of thought, not as 'constitutive' of reality. There is, however, a striking difference. For Kant the concept 'God,' while only 'regulative' from the standpoint of speculative reason, becomes virtually 'constitutive' when viewed from the standpoint of practical reason. But for Çankara there is no way of making the concept of a world-cause or a world-ground any more real than the phenomenal world itself. But the world-process, such as it is, serves as a sphere for the self-revelation of the highest Lord. 'The Self . . . reveals itself in a graduated series of beings, and so appears in forms of various dignity and power' (I, 1, 11). 'Wherever there is excess of power, and so on, there the Lord is to be worshipped.'[1] 'The highest Lord may, when he pleases, assume a bodily shape formed of Mâyâ, in order to gratify thereby his devout worshippers' (I, 1, 20). Such is Çankara's explanation and justification of the Indian theory of different incarnations.

4. We have then in the system of Çankara the absolute Brahman and Mâyâ standing over against each other, Brahman as pure thought and Mâyâ as the hypostasis of 'energy,' 'nature,' 'matter.' This at first sight looks like a speculative dualism, a transcendental rendering of the terms 'mind' and 'matter.' But Çankara saves his monism by making Mâyâ the synonym of *avidyâ* 'Nescience.' A word with reference to the analogous doctrine in Christian theology of 'the creation of the world out of nothing.' Its best scriptural support is perhaps found in such texts as 'By the word of the Lord were the heavens made; and all the host of them by *the breath of his mouth*. . . . For he spake, and, it was done; he commanded, and it stood fast.[2] The reference is clearly to Gen. I, 3: 'And God *said*, Let there be light: and there was light.' The thought of the Psalm is that God's power is so great that He can create as easily as a human being can speak or breathe. In like manner Çankara speaks of the highest Lord as having created all things 'in sport as it were, easily as a man sends forth his breath' (I, 1, 3). For

[1] Cf. *Gitâ*, X, 41. [2] Ps. XXXIII, 6, 9.

'although the creation of this world appears to us a weighty and difficult undertaking, it is mere play to the Lord, whose power is unlimited' (II, 1, 33). These passages both from the Hebrew and the Sanskrit suggest primarily the lack of effort with which God creates, and also possibly the unreality of the creation as compared with the immense reality of the Creator. But the Hebrew realism and the Indian doctrine of the identity of cause and effect would both seem to be against the last conjecture. However this may be, it is certain that for the mediæval theologians the world was created out of 'nothing' and that for Çankarâcârya the world is just Mâyâ 'illusion.' In the first system God and the world stand over against each other; in the second, Brahman and Mâyâ. The monism of both systems is saved by making the second term in each antithesis, namely the world and Mâyâ, derivative, secondary, nay in the deepest sense *unreal*.

B. Çankarâcârya and Râmânujâcârya.

Çankarâcârya lived in the eighth century (788–820 A. D.). In the twelfth century, however, another great exegete and theologian flourished, the famous *Râmânujâcârya*, likewise the author of a commentary on the Vedânta-Sûtras and the founder of a school of thought. The text of his commentary is not generally accessible, nor does the work exist in a complete translation, so far as I know. For the purpose in hand it is necessary to compare only the chief tenets of Râmânuja with the corresponding views of Çankara. The fundamental doctrines of the system of Râmânuja are presented with admirable brevity and clearness in Professor Thibaut's learned introduction to his translation of the Vedânta-Sûtras.[1] On the basis of this sketch the following points of difference between the two systems may be indicated:

1. As to the *unity* of Brahman, Râmânuja was the exponent of a qualified non-duality as opposed to the absolute non-duality of Çankara's system. Çankara conceived Brahman to be absolutely homogeneous. The objection that 'Brahman has in itself elements of manifoldness,' that 'as the tree has many

[1] SBE., Vol. XXXIV.

branches, so Brahman possesses many powers and emergies dependent on these powers,' and that 'unity and manifoldness are therefore both true' (the very position of Râmânuja, II, 1, 14) is mentioned only to be rejected on the ground that the phrase 'having its origin in speech' (Chând. Up., VI, 1, 4–6) declares the unreality of all effects. If we, on the basis of common sense, assume in the nature of Brahman 'an element of plurality' (II, 1, 31), it is only because of that innate and 'original' depravity of intellect by which we are compelled to view unity under the disguise of multiplicity. So Çankara taught. On the other hand, Râmânuja, as already hinted, held that multiplicity is not the foe of unity, but rather its ally and complement. The many somehow share in the reality of the One. There is no real antithesis between the One and the many. The unity of Râmûnuja is a concrete all-embracing unity rather than an abstract, naked, characterless unity such as Çankara taught. For Râmânuja the world is not unreal, but as composed of *acit* and *cit*, 'matter' and 'souls,' it constitutes the body of the Lord. The universe is one vast organism 'whose body nature is and God the soul.' The connection between Brahman and the world is real. Hence there is no distinction between a higher or unqualified and a lower or qualified Brahman. Hence, too, Brahman as the cause of a real world has the attributes of omniscience, omnipotence, omnipresence, etc., which are involved in such a relation. Moreover, there is a greater emphasis on the *moral* attributes of God than is displayed in the system of Çankara. "The Lord . . . is all-merciful ; his nature is fundamentally antagonistic to all evil."[1] In a word, the Brahman of Râmânuja is a personal God, who as the *Antaryâmin* or 'inner guide' (*Bṛh. Up.*, III, 7) is everywhere immanent both in nature and in man, permeating, animating and governing all things by his spirit.

2. As to the relation between Brahman and the individual soul, Râmânuja proclaimed a qualified identity as opposed to the absolute identity held by Çankara. For Çankara the individual soul is Brahman limited and disguised by the *upâdhis*, the offspring of Mâyâ. For Râmânuja, on the other hand, the in-

[1] Thibaut, SBE., Vol. XXXIV, p. xxviii.

dividual soul has a relative but nevertheless real existence. As a finite personality it is just as real in its own sphere as the infinite all-embracing personality of God. It is real because it shares in the reality of Brahman. Loss of separate personality through absorption in, or recognition of identity with, the highest Self is the ideal of Çankara. The preservation of personality and its assimilation to the nature and character of Brahman is the ideal of Râmânuja.

3. As regards cosmology both Râmânuja and Çankara admit the doctrine of a world-process consisting of evolution and dissolution. But for Çankara this process, while true from the standpoint of common-sense, is from the standpoint of Scripture and reason an illusion. For Râmânuja, however, it is a real development, a real modification of the substance of the Lord. Thus the theory of Mâyâ is accepted by Çankara, but rejected by Râmânuja.

Thus there are two types of the Vedânta, the Vedânta of Çankara and the Vedânta of Râmânuja. The former is abstract, idealistic and far removed from common sense; while the latter is concrete, realistic, and much nearer the standpoint of common sense. The watchword of the former is *unity without multiplicity*, all multiplicity being due to Mâyâ. The watchword of the latter is *unity in multiplicity*, the upâdhis being regarded as real forms of existence. The one proclaims a doctrine of identity; the other, a doctrine of emanation. The Brahman of Çankara is properly transcendent—as transcendent as the God of Deism; whereas the Brahman of Râmânuja is immanent, dwelling in all things as the *Antaryâmin* or 'inner guide.' Finally the system of Çankara represents Indian orthodoxy *par excellence*.

C. The Vedânta-Sûtras.

These consist of 555 brief aphorisms, mere 'threads' as it were on which to string 'the flowers of the Vedânta-passages' (I, 1, 2). Their purpose is to systematize the doctrine of the Upanishads. The Shorter Catechism of the Westminster Confession of Faith, so far as it is a résumé of the doctrines of the Bible, furnishes a modern analogue of the Indian Sûtras, although the latter do not proceed by way of question and answer. We may also compare the aphorisms of the *Novum Organum*, and the propositions in Spinoza's Ethics.

The Sûtra style is extremely condensed, but not otherwise intrinsically obscure. All writers agree, however, in affirming that there is an exception in the case of the two *Mîmâṁsâ-Sûtras*, the prior *Mîmâṁsâ* and the later *Mîmâṁsâ*, which systematize respectively the work-part (*karmakâṇḍa*) and the knowledge-part (*jnâñakâṇḍa*) of the Veda. Here, as Thibaut remarks, "Scarcely one single Sûtra is intelligible without a commentary" (pp. xiii–xiv). As an illustration of the combined brevity and obscurity of the Vedânta-Sûtras, we may cite Sûtra, I, 1, 3, *Çâstrayonitvât*, which may mean either 'Because (Brahman) is the source of Scripture,' or 'Because Scripture is the source (of the knowledge of Brahman).' Deussen thinks that the author (or authors) of the Vedânta-Sûtras was influenced by the desire to make the secret doctrine of the Upanishads as stated in the Sûtras inaccessible except through the oral comment of a qualified teacher.[1]

There are two ways of approaching the Vedânta-Sûtras: either by way of the Upanishads whose doctrine the Sûtras are supposed to sum up, or by way of the commentators, the earliest and most important of which are Çankarâcârya and Râmânujâcârya, both recognized doctors or teachers of the Vedânta as the epithet *Âcârya* indicates. It might be inferred on *a priori* grounds that the Sûtras set forth the same type of doctrine as is found in the Upanishads, since their sole aim is to reproduce in a systematic form the teaching thereof. But, not to mention the possibility of there being different types of doctrine in the Upanishads themselves, we have already seen that the two systems of Çankara and Râmânuja which differ on the most fundamental points, have been built upon the interpretation of the same Sûtras. Both interpretations can hardly be correct. We must look for the true meaning of the Sûtras either in the interpretation of Çankara or in that of Râmânuja, or possibly in neither. Professor Thibaut is the first to attempt to penetrate beyond the

[1] *Vedânta*, S. 28.

interpretations of the scholiasts to the meaning of the Sûtras themselves. This he does by instituting a careful comparison of the interpretations of Çankara with those of Râmânuja. His conclusions touching the type of Vedânta set forth in the Sûtras are exceedingly important. "I must give it as my opinion," he says, "that they do not set forth the distinction of a higher and lower knowledge of Brahman; that they do not acknowledge the distinction of Brahman and Içvara in Çankara's sense; that they do not hold the doctrine of the unreality of the world; and that they do not, with Çankara, proclaim the absolute identity of the individual and the highest Self."[1] These conclusions, startling as they are, can hardly be gainsaid by any one who carefully follows Professor Thibaut through his line of research and argumentation. The result to which we seem to be brought, then, is this, that while Râmânuja is the more faithful exponent of the Sûtras, Çankara is a more trustworthy guide to the meaning of the Upanishads. But this implies that the Sûtras do not in all respects adequately represent the doctrine of the Upanishads. How are we to account for this? A parallel from the history of Christian theology may help us here. Paulinism, *i. e.*, religion and theology as conceived by Paul and set forth in his Epistles, was the system under which the Apostolic Church mostly made its conquests throughout the Roman Empire. But soon degeneration set in. The theology of the middle ages was equal to the theology of Paul neither in religious depth nor in spiritual power. Finally the Reformation came with its cry of 'Back to the sources,' with its revival of the theology of Paul. The foremost representative of the Reformation on its theological and philosophical side was Calvin, just as the foremost representative, so far as we know, of the Hindu Revival, at least on its philosophical side, was Çankarâcârya. The two men have many things in common. Çankara is the exponent of the most speculative type of Vedântism, while Calvin represents the most speculative type of Christian theology. Both alike were great in exegesis as well as in theology, in fact they were great in theology partly because they were great in exegesis. Çankara wrote

[1] SBE., Vol. XXXIV, p. c.

commentaries in Sanskrit on most or all of the classic Upanishads, while Calvin expounded in Latin nearly the whole of the Christian Scriptures. Indian exegesis really begins with Çankara, just as modern Biblical exegesis begins with Calvin. But the fame of each rests primarily on constructive work in the field of theology. The '*monumentum aere perennius*' of Çankarâcârya is his *Bhâṣya* on the Vedânta-Sûtras, while Calvin's most famous work is the '*Institutio Christianæ Religionis.*' It is worth noticing that neither writer even in his most original and constructive work altogether forsook the rôle of a commentator. The *Bhâṣya* of Çankarâcârya is a commentary on the Vedânta-Sûtras, just as the '*Institutio*' of Calvin began as an exposition of the Ten Commandments, Lord's prayer, Apostles' Creed, and Sacraments. But the important thing is this, that Çankarâcârya, no less than Calvin, conducted his exposition in the light of a first-hand knowledge of all the sources involved. Put two things together, first the inherent obscurity of the Vedânta-Sûtras, and second Çankara's thorough knowledge of the Upanishads as the sources of the system expounded in the Sûtras, and it is easy to see how Çankara might interpret the system through the sources rather than the sources through the system. This conclusion is independent of the question whether he followed an exegetical and philosophical tradition or not. Râmânuja, however, seems to interpret the earlier sources through the later system.

It has already been remarked that it is doubtful whether the Sûtras adequately represent the doctrine of the Upanishads. It would be not at all strange, if they should not. The work of any creative period, whether in religion or in philosophy, is so unusual that the succeeding age always seems to be marked by degeneration. As instances of creative epochs take the period of the great prophets in Israel, of the classic Upanishads in India, of Socrates, Plato, and Aristotle in Greece, of Christ and His Apostles in the time of the New Testament, of Kant, Fichte, Schelling, and Hegel in modern times. All of these periods were succeeded by reaction. In each case the mountain peak of religious or philosophic intuition very soon sank down again nearly or quite to the old level. There are two main reasons why the Vedânta-Sûtras represent a less developed point of view than the Upanishads. First, as already pointed out in the discussion of the philosophy of the Upanishads, there was before very long a compromise between the religion of the Âtman and the religion of the Devas. As Thibaut says: "The pure doctrine of those ancient Brahmanical treatises underwent at a rather early period amalgamation with beliefs which most probably had sprung up in altogether different communities."[1] As a literary monument of such amalgamation Thibaut cites the Bhagavadgîtâ. But, secondly, every system of thought is determined not only by the positive content which it wishes to express, but also by the antagonisms which it is forced to meet. Now it is evident both from the text of the Vedânta-Sûtras and from the testimony of both Çankara and Râmânuja that the *Sâṁkhya* doctrine enjoyed especial prestige at the time of the composition of the Sûtras. In fact the great antagonist of the *Sûtrakâra* or author of the Sûtras was the *Sâṁkhyavâdin.* The *Sâṁkhya*, while in form a dualism affirming the eternal self-existence of both matter (*prakriti*) and souls (*purushas*), was nevertheless, so far as the origin of the world is concerned, a materialistic monism. Hence the doctrine of the *Sâṁkhya* was the natural foe of the spiritualistic monism of the Vedânta, Hence the duel between *Brahman* and *Pradhâna.* The Vedântin claimed that the cause of the world is the *intelligent* Brahman; the *Sâṁkhyavâdin*, that it is the *non-intelligent* pradhâna. According to the one the world-ground is by nature intelligent: according to the other intelligence is a late product of evolution. It is remarkable that the system of Schopenhauer who professed such unbounded admiration for the Upanishads, is more nearly akin to the materialistic side of the *Sâṁkhya* than to the Vedânta of either Çankara or Râmânuja. We have in the conflict between *Sâṁkhya* and *Vedânta* the Indian phase of the eternal struggle between materialism and spiritualism. The Sûtrakâra felt that the refutation of the *Sâṁkhya* doctrine of a non-intelligent pradhâna was virtually the 'refutation of all heresies.' At the time he wrote it was probably by no means certain what

[1] *Op. cit.*, p. cxxvi.

the issue would be. But—and this is the important point—the very fierceness of the antagonism which the Sûtrakâra was compelled to meet could not have been without influence on his mode of statement. The hypothesis of a non-intelligent principle (*pradhâna*) as the cause of the world *required* the counter hypothesis of an intelligent principle (Brahman), likewise conceived as the real cause of a real world. This is the position of the Sûtrakâra according to all probability as well as the position of Râmânuja.

A comparatively realistic interpretation of Brahman on the part of the Sûtrakâra was also demanded by the antithesis of Buddhism. Buddha was in a sense an Indian Hume. As the philosophy of Hume is simply the philosophy of Berkeley with God left out, so "Buddhism is the philosophy of the Upanishads with Brahman left out."[1] As a result the system of Buddha was almost as pure a nihilism as the system of Hume. This, I say, is an additional reason why the Sûtrakâra should have conceived Brahman as the real cause of a real world. Buddhism was alive in India in the days of the Sûtrakâra, but it was virtually dead when Çankara wrote. Hence Çankara could revive the older idealism of the Upanishads, since the later idealism of Buddha no longer stood in the way.

The date of the Vedânta-Sûtras is uncertain. All we are absolutely sure of is that they fall between the time of the oldest Upanishads (perhaps 400 B. C.) and the time of Çankarâcârya (800 A. D.). But the Sûtrakâra refers to earlier teachers, *e. g.*, *Âçmarathya*, *Audulomi*, *Jaimini*, *Bâdari et al.*, in such a way as to make it pretty clear that the Sûtras occupy, as Thibaut says, "*a strictly central position*, summarizing, on the one hand, a series of early literary essays extending over many generations, and forming, on the other hand, the head spring of an ever broadening activity of commentators as well as virtually independent writers."[2] The Vedânta-Sûtras, then, will hardly be earlier than the beginning of the Christian era and possibly later even than that.

[1] Gough, *Upanishads*, p. 187.
[2] Introduction to *SBE.*, vol. XXXIV, p. xii.

If time had permitted, a chapter might have been added on the work of the later theologians, the authors of dogmatic treatises such as the *Vedânta-Sâra* the *Vedânta-Paribhâṣâ* and the *Pañcadaçî.* These carry on the work of Çankarâcârya and are related to him much as the later Protestant scholastics Turretinus, Amesius and Zanchius are related to Calvin. In a word, they render the abstractions of Çankara in still more abstract terms. An able criticism of the Vedânta of the later theologians is to be found in Pandit Nehemiah Goreh's Rational Refutation of the Hindu Philosophical Systems as translated by Dr. Fitz-Edward Hall.

The systems of Çankarâcârya and Râmânujâcârya are related to each other, somewhat as Calvanism is related to Arminianism. Calvanism is religious rationalism. Arminianism is religious empiricism. The one construes theology from the Godward side; the other, from the manward side. The one is the more logical; the other, the more human. A similar difference in point of view separates the systems of Çankara and Râmânuja from each other. There is, however, an important qualification to be made. Râmánuja construes the theology of the Upanishads, as summarized in the Sûtras, from only *one* point of view, which may be called (although not quite accurately) the point of view of experience. Çankara, on the other hand, adopts a double point of view, the standpoint of Râmânuja as well as his own proper standpoint. Dr. Shedd, my honored teacher in theology, is reported to have once said in the course of conversation: "The Bible is a Calvinistic book," and then apparently as an afterthought, "but it has a good many Arminian texts in it." This is exactly the position of Çankara with reference to the Upanishads. For him the doctrine of the Upanishads was the doctrine of the higher Brahman, and yet he saw clearly that many texts refer to the lower Brahman. So by his doctrine of a higher and a lower Brahman, the Brahman of philosophic intuition and the Brahman of religious belief and experience, he sought to do justice to both classes of texts. With Çankara's distinction between the higher and the lower Brahman we may compare Spinoza's distinction between the god of philosophy as expounded in the *Ethica*, the object of a passionless '*amor intellectualis*,' and the god of theology or revelation as described in the *Tractatus Theologico-Politicus*. It may be doubted whether the distinction between a higher and a lower Brahman in Çankara's sense is formally recognized in the Upanishads. But that it is implied in some of their noblest utterances seems to me fairly clear. At any rate, as Thibaut says, "the adoption of that distinction furnishes the interpreter with an instrument of extraordinary power for reducing to an orderly whole the heterogeneous material presented by the old theosophic treatises. . . . It is not only more pliable, more capable of amalgamating heterogeneous material than other systems, but its fundamental doctrines are manifestly in greater harmony with the essential teaching of the Upanishads than those of the other Vedântic systems."[1] To venture on another comparison, the monistic Vedânta of Çankara bears about the same relation to the qualified monistic Vedânta of Râmânuja that supralapsarian Calvinism bears to sublapsarian Calvinism.

In the Rig-Veda Brahman is simply 'hymn' or 'prayer.' In the system of Çankara it is the absolute, the unthinkable. Between these two limits we have the following scheme of development. Brahman, the word, is, on the one hand, objectified, and so becomes as it were incarnate in the world of nature. It is, on the other hand, '*subjectified*,' so to speak, and conceived as the indwelling reason or self of things. The last step in the process of abstraction is to separate Brahman from everything knowable or thinkable.

Our task is done. The primary aim has been, not to controvert, but to understand. An objective attitude has been maintained throughout. Criticism should wait upon historical exposition, and not complicate its processes by premature objections. The development of the doctrine of Brahman is interesting not only from the point of view of Indian history, philosophy, and theology, but also for the light which it throws on the psychology of the Indian mind.

[1] *Op. cit.*, pp. cxxiii, cxxiv.